PUBLIC

SPEAKING

HOW TO CONQUER YOUR FEAR AND BOOST YOUR CREDIBILITY

Melissa Kalan

All enquiries should be made to
info@arma-revenuemanagement.com

Creator: KALAN, Melissa

Title: PUBLIC SPEAKING – HOW TO CONQUER YOUR FEAR AND BOOST YOUR CREDIBILITY

ISBN: 978-0-6450295-0-5

Published by: Australian Revenue Management Association Pty Ltd

Website: www.arma-revenuemanagement.com

© Melissa Kalan

1st edition – November, 2020

Disclaimer

This book is a course offered by the Australian Revenue Management Association Pty Ltd via their online course academy.

To obtain certification for this course you will need to complete the online course and assessments to receive your certificate of completion.

This book is intended as a general guide only and can't ensure you will be successful as a public speaker even if you follow all of the advice. To the maximum extent permitted by law, the author and publisher disclaim all responsibility and liability to any person, arising directly or indirectly from any person taking or not taking action based on the information in this publication.

For my family who raised me with the belief to always "walk tall and stand proud."

For my husband who always encourages me to chase my dreams and just go for it!

For my mentors, thank you for your trust and belief.

And for my children, never give up because anything is actually possible.

PUBLIC SPEAKING

HOW TO CONQUER YOUR FEAR AND BOOST YOUR CREDIBILITY

Contents

INTRODUCTION

WHY I CREATED THIS BOOK

"If you can speak, you can influence. If you can influence, you can change lives." — Rob Brown

I magine for a moment you're at the pearly gates of heaven. It's nice as far as heaven is concerned, but your regrets have also come along with you. What is the one thing you always wanted to do? What did you miss out on?

After speaking with countless individuals, either as their coach or mentor, I've noticed a trend to steer away from challenging life aspects. It could be procrastination that holds you back, or even more than that; it could be that you have a fear of doing something. Whatever your blocking emotion might, it is often rooted in the unknown.

One of the biggest challenges as a business owner or leader is to grab the attention of your market, showcase your products and services to your prospective customers, and then get them to buy. So, let me ask you this one thing: "Do you believe that you have enough brand authority to sell your products at present?"

If you answered yes, then you're on your way to creating what you desire with your business or career. If you said no, maybe I can help you to build that brand authority. Many people follow the standard model of doing so using SEO, hiring a public relations manager, and likely spending countless dollars on something you don't need. I will show you how I build brand authority for myself, allowing me to launch various courses and services that keep-on selling.

Where shall we start? Perhaps at the beginning would be best.

My name is Melissa Kalan, and I've been using public speaking as my secret weapon to gain new clients and build authority for my service offers. If you picked up this book, I'm guessing you would like to do the same, and that's where I can help you.

My own business started with a desire to teach people. Call it an innate sense or a calling, but I always found teaching and helping others was very fulfilling. Now, my niche area of expertise was in revenue and yield management. What exactly is that? It is the discipline where I help business owners across various business models with a perishable product, optimize their assets. That was one aspect, but what I noticed and was a game-changer for me was the lack of available education and speakers on this topic.

That was perhaps the turning point for me as an entrepreneur. It made me see that yes, I wanted to reach more people even before the explosion of online education. I knew that gaining credibility as a thought leader on this topic was essential to have global leverage and would be something that would help to sell my courses. Yet, what appeared to hold me back was that I had never done any public speaking before, and guess what? Teaching = public speaking!

We've all seen reputable courses that draw us in to make that purchase, so I wanted to be seen as a powerful brand, and I also wanted to gain both credibility and respect in my industry. Perhaps you can relate.

This meant growing my brand since I was the leader of this business. Yet, the only people talking publicly at events at the time were industry software vendors. I guess they knew the power of public speaking earlier on as a sales tool, only for them, they wanted to sell their software. It was their main priority, so they made a vendor presentation, which was unappealing to the audience but it was their only option. The audience felt sold to rather than educated and I truly believe if you can educate and provide real value then the sales flow on naturally. Observing this was the catalyst for me. It made me see that I also had a product, however, it was an educational product. It was an educational resource that could help people reach their goals and make more money. So, I had to learn many of the speaker trade tricks on my own through experimenting and observing and get ready for a public speaking opportunity, and that's when it happened.

After I had made a launch for my business, an invitation arrived for me. I was invited to speak at a conference. Then it happened again, and to my surprise, a couple more times after that. Can you imagine it? I was asked so many times that it made me feel confident enough to speak in front of any crowd, and I'm guessing you'd love to do the same.

Looking back at those early presentations, I cringe even though I was well-received and I can see how much I've grown and evolved in my career. My skill itself has improved and shown me that public speaking is a skill, not only that, but it is a high-value skill that keeps you on your toes, always learning and growing, and very rewarding too!

So that's my story of how I met and fell in love with public speaking. It's funny how it happened when it was only my goal to use my online business to educate and coach. Before I started face-to-face workshops I, used to freeze at the thought of running an all-day training session – how would I fill in all that time? I remember how easy it became for me after lots of practice and where there were 8-hour workshops where I did not need to reference my notes. That is when the true magic as a presenter happens.

Perhaps you're in that place right now, you're reading my story, and you hope to become more proficient in public speaking. I was there in the early stages of my career, where it seemed so scary. I had nervous tension and the sweaty palms that come with it, and you know many people tell you to imagine everyone naked. From experience, I can say that it doesn't work. But I had to learn that through practice!

I learned an important trick is that you don't need to mix up your material too much when discussing the same topic, since you mostly will always have different people each time. In this way, it helps you ease the stress that comes with presenting something new. It pays to remember that for new people, it's the first time they hear your material. I'm trying to get at that when you do the same material repeatedly; you get so good at sharing your message you become confident and have clarity on stage, your experience shows through and you can wow your audience.

People are naturally drawn to both your confidence and competence. This is the magic spot I always say, where you are free to add in spontaneous stories, news events, and generally mix things up without the fear of looking unprofessional your skills start to take off on a new level.

There will also come a time in your public speaking career where your experience and practice help the audience respect you, and again, they might even consider you a subject matter expert. The better you get, the more opportunities fall into your lap, and that's precisely what happened with me. I was invited to the arena of panel moderating which takes on a whole new public speaking challenge. I have also been invited as a guest on CEO panels with no pre-questions or prep time allowed! Now to pull this off well, you really need to have had a lot of public speaking practice.

Yet these opportunities will come if you remain consistent and persistent over time and always strive to deliver value and be engaging and professional to work with.

You might be wondering if these speaking engagements were unpaid. Well, honestly, earlier on, they were not paid, but over time I started to gain respect and build credibility as a thought leader, and I was able to charge for keynote speaking services at certain events.

I could also see the potential of being a thought leader, and I wondered: "What If I could run my own event for my market, bring in and connect with valuable speakers and be the MC of my own conference?'

I decided to lead live-in-person events as one of my marketing tools, bringing in more revenue to my business and again raising my profile and credibility in this space. I found quickly that your success in this area heavily relies on the program, topics, and the quality of speakers you bring on board.

I discovered that just because someone was a subject matter expert did not necessarily make them a successful event speaker. Also, in my particular niche market, balancing the agenda with male and female presenters was difficult, not because there weren't enough experts in the field, but rather, the fear of speaking mainly to women corporate professionals became very evident quickly. Yet, I'm always persistent at encouraging more women take the stage too.

You may be wondering why I've taken you down a winding path as we've discussed my story, public speaking, and how I've used it in business. The goal here is to show you the outcome of gaining public speaking skills for your business or career. That's the core of this book, to provide you a practical approach to public speaking and to give you real-life information and checklists that you can apply. This book essentially is one of our popular courses and your guiding resource if you crave the desire to gain confidence and speak in front of an audience.

What if you're relatively new to public speaking? Well, this course in a book will be your perfect companion that will encourage you to speak up more in meetings and eventually start giving presentations that will surprise and excite your organization. Additionally, if you're an entrepreneur who just launched their business, and you want to work on your brand, then this course in a book has the tools to help you gain credibility as a speaker. If there's one thing I've learned as a public speaker, it's that you can command a revenue for your time and knowledge and become a highly sought-after speaker who is also well-paid.

By the end of this book, if you take action and follow-through, you will wonder how you ever felt pressure speaking in public before. You'll think on your feet, mastering your thoughts and ideas, and then sharing that in a concise and inspiring manner.

At this point, let's take a moment to pause and think about what you hope to achieve personally from reading this book. Also, note down what's currently holding you back. Keep this note as we will return to this at a later stage in this book.

For now, it's time to dig into this resource that will give you the persuasive edge in your industry or corporation.

Let's get into the first chapter…

CHAPTER 1

THE POWER OF PUBLIC SPEAKING

"Public Speaking is a skill that can be studied, polished, perfected.
Not only can you get good at it, but you can also get damn good at it,
and it makes a heck of a difference"
— Tom Peters

Looking back in history, we've seen that public speaking could change the world in which we live. It is powerful and helpful to use in both our business and personal lives. As time has passed, many of the best leaders of our time have given us some of the most memorable speeches on the planet. They used their speaking ability to ignite inspiration, passion and sparked a movement.

Not only could they move individuals, but they could also inspire national and global change for the better. The power of speaking is in how you can impact your audience and if you leave them better than you found them. Do you know an inspiring leader who has helped you on your journey? Maybe it was a post they shared on social media, or perhaps it was a video you saw. The fact remains it was memorable, and for that moment, you decided to feel inspired and take action.

This tradition of the exemplary orator can be consistently brought to the fore. We need only reach our minds and think of the most iconic speeches of history, which was the Tilbury speech that Queen Elizabeth I shared and how that changed history. Even though the address was made in 1588, we could see how Queen Elizabeth I was a master of words and spurred her troops on against the Spaniards at the time.

And of course, you may have heard of the ultimate speech "Quit India" by Gandhi, which resulted in England allowing India's freedom after decades of rule. Gandhi was an excellent, calm, and influential speaker, and that connection created a less violent world.

Or how about the revolutionary speech that rallied so many people towards a fair and free America. Yes, it was Martin Luther King, Jrs' "I have a dream" speech. To this day, we share this speech to create change for the world over and avoid segregation, hate and prejudice.

The common thread with all of these great orators would be that they stood for something greater themselves. They had a cause that they 100% believed in, and they wanted to share their message to help that cause. Their commitment was focused, and we believed every word they said because they were filled with passion and sharing this through their speeches.

Yet, before you get to that point of public speaking, it pays to remember that even these brilliant speakers had to start somewhere. They failed on stage and messed up their words. They were not born perfect. When you understand that mastering the craft of public speaking, it's clear that this skill is more than a set of spoken words said to the world at large. Far from it, it's about targeting your messaging and using all your resources to make it stick or hit home. It's about honing your craft by improving how you speak, sharing unique ideas, using the right tone, and bringing it all together with just the right delivery. If this batch of ingredients works, then you will be a maker of change. You will influence the difference in the world for your biggest causes that you are passionate about.

Let's pause at this point and ask the question of: "How will learning public speaking help your career or business?"

It's really about shifting the concept of public speakers and how they operate. Gone are the days where you deliver a speech and hope for people to find. You have to build a community and create meaningful, authentic relationships with your ideal audience. These relations will help you make adequate space for your public speaking business to start. Yet this can also be applied to your brand; whereas you begin learning how to communicate your message succinctly and influencing people to take action, your brand will start to see traction.

That's the reason podcasts and video have seen a massive uptick in the last few years as people realize they can use video to grab more people's attention and bring them to their products or service.

Maybe if you've been in the business world or had a career for a few decades, you'd know the term "death by PowerPoint," and it merely means that people don't want to see boring, lifeless presentations made by a less than charismatic speaker. They want to be entertained and educated at the same time, so you have to speak their language.

In this way, yes, you will be presenting your ideas, and you can do so by using your speaking skills to maximum effect. The truth is that when inadequate presentations are used, you waste both your viewer and your time.

More than that, you can still get by with a poor presentation, provided you, as the speaker, can show competence, confidence, and charisma in your approach. We've indeed reached a point where business leaders' communication and speaking style can make or break their business. Not only can the public speaking you do be applied externally but also within your own company. If you have a disengaged workforce, what better way to reignite them with your new public speaking skills? They may be so surprised that you chose to speak humanely, kindly, and with a sense of humor. Eventually, they start following suit, and your culture will improve in your company.

Yes, I will also be sharing more benefits and adding useful ways to share your message too. For now, please consider that business and other individuals are riddled by fear. It's the fear of judgment or the fear that it will remove them from the roll call for success. Yet the fear of speaking is experienced by almost every speaker I know. It's not a matter of being born with the ability to speak publicly but how you did something to improve your situation. The action will eventually be the reason you make it.

The power of public speaking is immense, and every day the opportunities increase if you're willing to short circuit and pause your fear. I'm going to show you how in the next chapter, I want to show you what you're missing out on when you don't go all-in on public speaking for your business.

CHAPTER 2

THE 17 BENEFITS OF PUBLIC SPEAKING

"The worst speech you'll ever give will be far better than the one you never give." – Fred Miller

As a public speaker, I'm always amazed at the benefits I see in my career. And I'm not talking about the perks like engaging with the top minds of our generation. It's more than that; there is an enormous amount of personal and professional growth that flows on to all aspects of your life.

Did you know that it's a common misconception that being a public speaker is all about the actual stage event? There is so much that goes on behind the scenes that might even surprise you and we will explore that a little later.

In this chapter, I'd first like to take you behind the scenes with me as a public speaker and show you all the benefits I've seen for my students, my network, and yes, even myself when it comes to being a public speaker.

1. You Will Improve Career Opportunities

When you improve your public speaking confidence this is particularly of benefit in your place of work. No longer will you be afraid to speak up in meetings, promote your idea and sit in fear of being put on the spot.

Instead, you will relish the chance to show up and contribute, showcasing your professionalism and charisma. I would even say that your improved public speaking skills will give you the edge over other candidates in interviews.

More employers seek critical thinking skills, empathy, poise, and professionalism in the candidates, these would be considered a high-value skill set and are very much skills expected from quality public speakers.

2. There may be confidence boosts

Confidence can come in many forms. Maybe it's finally applying for that promotion at work, or finally making that call you've been dreading.

Understand also that public speaking can enhance your self-confidence.

The little steps towards mastery of your fear and overcoming those insecurities are enough to make you feel empowered and excited to do more stress-inducing tasks!

The feedback loop that comes from connecting with your audience will be invaluable. What will it do? It will make you see that connecting with large and small audiences shows that you have valuable experiences and ideas to share. Your work matters, and that might even give you a sense of purpose.

I've seen dramatic shifts in the confidence level you gain from speaking to small groups to then graduating to larger groups, and the benefits will keep rolling in.

Keep in mind, you may always feel some sense of nervousness, and that's normal. The game-changer is that you will learn how to deal with the fears that come up when you publicly speak, categorize them, and then move forward. That's how you will essentially turn your challenges into improvement milestones.

3. Enhancement of your critical thinking skills

Your critical thinking skills often come up when you need to look at various angles of a problem present at work or in your business. Now, in the past, you may have struggled to think critically through a problem, and it may even have impacted you while doing interviews resulting in you failing to secure the job. But it can change once you start to employ your public speaking skills.

So, I always recommend public speaking for individuals in all areas of life who want to improve their critical thinking skills. Remember that when you write a speech it draws upon so many aspects of your thought process. You always have to be thinking audience analysis (what they need from me) and how to keep them engaged, right up to leaving a lasting impression with your closing sentence.

The trick here is that you must understand that it's not enough to have just a message; you also need to find a way to use the information to educate and guide your audience, engage and inspire them. How can you help your audience understand your message and leave wanting to talk about your session for days after?

Those questions have to be solved, and that's where critical thinking comes in. Once you start thinking critically about your speaking style and your audience's alignment, you will find ways to improve your thinking skills, planning, creativity and innovation skills and your general communication style that will benefit you both at work and at home.

4. You will seek out more personal development opportunities

Personal development is about the improvement of yourself in a variety of areas in your life. It means taking a step back and choosing better mental models, better learning approaches, and yes, even investing in your education. One area you will see your personal development bloom would be in how you communicate either professionally or personally.

That's why communication skills are listed as crucial for success, and when you improve in this area, it will be directly linked as a benefit derived from public speaker.

In my experience, preparing a speech forces you to take a step back, think critically about effective and different ways to communicate. Sometimes you have to think of fresh ways to communicate the same point over and over and adapt your style to your audience.

When you are moving down the journey as a public speaker, you evaluate every aspect of your communication personality and improve it all of the time.

5. You will be able to communicate in most situations

Understanding how your communication style affects people will certainly make you think about the impact of your words relative to your body language and tone and any mismatches that can occur. Perhaps you may begin to understand why people avoid you at times because of subconscious communication habits or you may see why people find you more friendly and useful to be around than another.

This something you learn as you understand and observe the general speaking framework. For example, when you write a speech, you must always contemplate the best structure, tone, and body language to communicate it in the way you intended it to be received by your audience.

This habit of critical thinking can seep into all areas of your life and help you communicate effectively and build better relationships through these interpersonal skills. Keep in mind that relationships, social and work situations always require you to share ideas and communicate well with others.

6. Upgrade and update your social connections

Generally, when you enter the world of public speaking, you start to attend more speaking events, and that's where you can meet many people and have people reach out that were inspired by your speech, presentation or discussion.

As you advance towards securing public speaking engagements, you will also expand your network with others who may be into what you are. I've often found that the best way to make new connections is right after your presentation when people will come over to chat about something. You'll also build good habits for engaging right back with these contacts who may be your next business lead or offer you another speaking opportunity because they liked what they saw.

After your speech, it's also an opportunity to go ahead and get connected with the audience, answering questions seeking fresh and unique takes on your topic. More than that, your social presence will grow as you share your contact details in your slides or if the organizers do it for you. Suppose you have a website, you can direct audience members to find more information there. One key tip I can share is that you must undoubtedly reach out to your fellow presenters if you are part of a speaking event. Congratulate them on how they did and share what you loved about their speech. Or you ask them how it went if you missed their presentation.

Public speaking is a gateway to many social and ultimately business opportunities. There are lots of options for networking when public speaking, so aim to be strategic in your approach.

7. Achieve a high leave of personal satisfaction with your life

Public speaking is a common fear, with most people admitting to feeling scared of public speeches at one stage in their lives. Studies show that on average nearly 73% of society have challenges and fear related to public speaking. It makes sense why this statistic is so high because giving a speech might bring up fears you didn't know you had. You may even notice that fears and insecurities multiply as your speech time draws closer. You ask yourself in your head: "Imagine if I don't remember my words?" "What happens if I can't keep it together and lose my connection with the audience?"

Eventually, even after all these questions and stress-inducing moments, you make it through the moment, and the audience loves it! Without public speaking or putting yourself in front of those people, you would never have known you could inspire people. Public speaking can help show you what's possible and can push you to do many other things in your life that you may not have achieved or even attempted otherwise. What starts as a stress inducing situation can turn into a personal victory!

8. Grow your network

Nowadays, when we discuss expanding your professional network, people immediately assume it must be through a platform like LinkedIn. Yes, LinkedIn is vital to showcasing your skills and leveraging it to grow your network. However, the benefit of public speaking is that you will suddenly find that more people want to engage with you when you speak at an event and so will their contacts and so on.

Speaking at an event is also a learning opportunity for you, not only to get you get to attend and hear great content, you can also meet the other great speakers, pick their brains for tips while you're there and observe how they work the stage, dazzle and engage the audience and structure their presentation slides.

9. Learn new techniques of persuasion

Persuasion tools are not only for negotiations and high-speed company takeovers. In fact, being persuasive is undoubtedly a useful tool to have. You can certainly build this skill as you grow into the role of a public speaker.

The art of public speaking can be a strong catalyst for change, as we saw in chapter 1. We saw how it could bring people together and focus on hard-hitting topics like prejudice, climate change, and leadership in the future. This opportunity puts you in the driving seat to help people make positive changes in their lives. Even if it's just one person you impact, you've created a better space in the world for growth.

Who knows how many more people can be influenced by your powerful future public speaking moments?

10. Step into a leadership role with your newfound skills

If you've always wanted to take on leadership roles in your career but were too afraid to speak in front of people, then becoming a better public speaker can help you in this area. No longer will you feel the need to let others do the talking for you. You'll clearly express what you want to say and provide inspiration and passion along the way.

Not only will you be able to organize your thoughts and words coherently, but you'll give others the courage to do the same. In my experience, I've seen individuals who would never have stood up in front of one person and say a speech, but now they command stages, and I would argue they lead that stage and inspire people along the way.

Taking a stand and making a commitment to speaking is so powerful. You commit yourself to learn the tools to update people's mindsets.

Mastering this skill, changing hearts, and learning to influence people are at the core of your leadership journey. Of course, you can start small and show your leadership skills through persuasion and charisma, but soon you will command large stages and audiences where you'll drive change using your public speaking ability, and for that, your public speaking skills are vital.

11. Learn high-performance skills

In leadership courses I have written we often focus on this crucial idea of leveraging skills to be high performing. As a public speaker, high performance is all about what you do on that stage. It's the connection you have with the audience and how you can leverage their engagement, deliver value and leave them inspired and wanting more.

Yet it takes training, practice, patience, dedication and a will to succeed. It would help if you studied public speaking mechanics and even study various disciplines like acting. You'll even need to be a master storyteller who can weave in and out of the narrative. It's incredible how you pull skills from a variety of disciplines to improve your public speaking skills. And it doesn't ever stop, you will always be learning new skills, and these tools will become your high-performance skills which you master.

12. Expand your vocabulary and speaking proficiency

Most adults speaking their native language possess up to 30,000 words in their vocabulary; however, you'll far exceed that as a public speaker. You'll also get to know the effects of many single words, and how just one small change can amplify the mood in the room or break it. Even more important is that you won't need filler words (uhm and like are good examples). When you remove those filler words, you will feel more competent in your speech, and it will push you to read and research more and more so that you can extend your vocabulary. I remember watching myself back in the early days and realizing just how many times I said "uhm" without even realizing it – not so much because I didn't have the right word to use, but rather as a nervous habit or feeling that I needed to stretch out the time – I soon discovered that you don't need to do that at all but it can be a very hard habit to break and one that I always keep front of mind no matter how many speaking engagements I have done.

13. Limit fear of unexpected speaking engagements

Maybe you've had the experience of being called to make a speech suddenly at a work event or family gathering, and suddenly all the air leaves your body. It's an all too familiar feeling that everyone has felt at some point in their life.

However, as you move towards your goal of becoming a more confident public speaker, you will not hesitate to step forwards at family events or work gatherings. You may even be the go-to person to make a speech when everyone is stepping back into the shadows. And trust me no-one feels good the very first time they make any sort of speech in public! We all cringe when we watch ourselves back and wished the ground would open up and swallow us.

However, in time you'll stop constantly worrying about this at work events just in case your manager asks you to say something or Aunty Joan calls on you at the next family gathering. You'll realize how fun it can be to entertain an audience using your expert speaking skills and rock it with confidence.

14. Love the joy of debate

You may remember speech day at school or where you had to participate in a debate to help you get a good grade? School students are still tortured with at least having to give one speech during their time at school, and trust me that used to be me at school – feeling "tortured" at the thought of it and in the moment. The good news is that even if you feel awful during your school years, you can learn to find the joy later in your life. Not everyone has to debate at school anymore, often this is left to a debating team, however, as a public speaker, you'll find controversial discussions more comfortable and even exciting at times too.

Training in debating can help you understand various sides of a problem and bring both viewpoints to your audience. This certainly makes people view you as a more holistic speaker and thinker. My tip would be to do as much research as possible and look at both sides of the topic so you can anticipate the angle your opponents might approach the debate with and work on ideal responses.

No matter what type of speaking presentation you are giving – research often and read widely on the subject matter.

15. Helps you drive positive and lasting change

Which option would command your attention? Someone who sends you an email or who is having a face to face conversation with you? The reality is that the person speaking will always be better placed to convince or influence others than an email or a text, although the power of the written word is very influential too – but that's another topic on copywriting.

The more people you engage with face-to-face either in-person or virtually, the more chance you can fast forward change. Think about an audience of 300 people that might be or become influencers in their industries and they may then go and share your message with their contacts and teams. The power of this exponential impact cannot be emphasized enough. More so, if you have a near and dear cause, you can use your platform to gain support and improve that situation. The possibilities are endless!

16. Be a better listener

Listening skills are often the most common skills employers look for when hiring. Why is it so common? Mostly because it tends to be why many processes don't hit the mark in the working world. People don't listen, and it seriously derails projects and momentum in business. A good public speaking can draw attention from a group of people that are not prone to listen at all, this can be of great benefit to an employer and also a fresh challenge for many public speakers to adapt their engagement style to ensure attention is given.

You also have to train yourself to listen closely all of the time, as it gives you the chance to embrace other points of views, learn from them and possibly incorporate into future speeches by way of example or use as an interesting story to help convey a message. Any real like examples you can draw upon really resonate with your audience. I often write notes in my phone or carry a notebook or send myself an email with ideas as I come across them, often at random times like at school pick-up, on a client call, while watching television or in the middle of the night so I have new material to draw on when the next speaking engagement comes along.

17. Grow and leverage your own business

You might be at that point where you are seeking other ways to feel engaged, especially if your work or job is not inspiring you. Maybe it's a business you've started or are thinking of starting then it helps to know that as you improve your speaking skills by investing in yourself and your learning, like taking this step to read this book then you will begin to feel confident to put yourself out there for events. What happens then? You'll book more events, and people will remember you and start to think of you as an authoritative figure in your area of expertise.

You'll find yourself getting new clients from the audience or even people who saw you speak and referred you to their company decision-makers. This will lead to more speaking opportunities in the long run or client work. The reality is that people want to do business with those they like and can put their trust in. One of the fastest ways to make people feel like they know you and trust you even if they have never met you is growing your credibility and reputation as a recognized thought leader in your area of expertise.

While this is not merely meant to be a list of benefits, it's more than that. I wanted to show you that when you leave your comfort zone and start getting into public speaking, it will bring change and new opportunities you never thought were possible. Will it be nerve-wracking at first? Yes, it will be, but you will quickly learn to manage those nerves and challenge them in a better way.

Of course, this is the point at which you have understood the foundations of public speaking and the benefits this new world of engagements and connections can bring you both on a professional and personal level, yet I always recommend that you crawl before you can walk and walk before you run! So, take each step with intention and make sure you fully grasp the previous step before you move to the next.

Public speaking is a life long journey that develops over time and like any skill needs to be practiced to keep you at the top of your game.

So now you are reading to think about your own personal learning goals and jump on in to our expert course content all wrapped up in this book resource for you. As I said earlier, there is so much that goes on in the preparation phase that enables you to shine in your moment on "stage" in whatever shape or form that moment might be.

To make things more straightforward for you, I also created checklists included in various topics and a "next steps" guide which I'll share in this book's final chapter.

So, let's get started…I'm excited for you!
Melissa x

YOUR PERSONAL LEARNING GOALS

This "course in a book" has been designed as a valuable learning resource for those in positions where they must speak in front of audiences and is also suitable for those who are relatively new speakers who want some encouragement to speak up in meetings or who want some training before they begin making presentations on behalf of the organization.

Perhaps you're an entrepreneur who has launched their own business and want to grow your profile and personal brand, then public speaking is a fast way to gain credibility. Successful public speakers can also command revenue for their time and knowledge shared and highly sought-after speakers can command top dollars. After all, you become the major draw card that helps the event planner sell tickets and make money and you should be compensated accordingly.

Whether you are speaking live at in-person events, or online in virtual training sessions and conferences public speaking makes many people frozen with fear and panic.

Speaking under pressure, or thinking on your feet, means being able to quickly organize your thoughts and ideas, and then being able to convey them meaningfully to your audience to modify their attitudes or behavior. It applies to formal speeches as well as everyday business situations.

It requires presence of mind, goal orientation, adaptation, and judgment. It also requires differentiating between oral and written communications.

This learning resource is aimed at improving your skills and learning some new techniques which will give you the persuasive edge when you are making a presentation, fielding difficult

questions, or presenting complex information. Take a moment to think of what your personal learning objectives and fears are and feel free to jot them down below.

CHAPTER 3

PREPARE TO PLAN AND UNDERSTAND

"All speaking is public speaking, whether it's to one person or one thousand" – Roger Love

Any form of public speaking can feel like a **pressured situation.** This first chapter will focus on how to build skills for dealing with unsympathetic audiences. It addresses some of your worst fears about being on the spot and the fear of what if they ask a question at the end I can't answer?

This first chapter presents techniques to organize ideas in pressure situations or when no advance preparation time is available. The core of this chapter is about developing thinking strategies which guide our ability to analyze, organize, and present ideas. At the end of this chapter you will be able to quickly organize and structure a presentation, deliver a convincing message without speaker's notes, and provide sound and convincing answers to the most difficult questions.

We're going to use a technique that is used throughout the world, and yet remains unknown to most people. This technique has been adapted by large speaker training organizations such as Toastmasters International. To plan each speaking opportunity, whether it is two minutes or an hour, we use an **opening, body, and closing.** We stress that you prepare as much as possible, yet still allow for flexibility. Then you practice, practice, and practice.

There is an old saying: "Be careful what you think, for these become your words. Be careful of your words, for they become your actions. Be careful of your actions, for they become your habits. Be careful of your habits, for they become your character. Be careful of your character, for your character becomes your destiny."

All we really need to get from this is that **clear thinking will usually result in clear speaking**, and generally we become clearer at what we want to say as we think and plan our approach.

So that our clear thinking is evident to others, it's important that we are perceived as organized and prepared. That means having an opening, a body, and a closing, when we are presenting or responding to a question.

For people who want to get ahead in life (which most of us do!), developing the ability to speak with clarity is one of the greatest talents we can cultivate. One way to get clarity is to write our thoughts down on paper or to work them out on a computer. A second way is to practice speaking with clarity. Perhaps the best technique is to combine these two: write our thoughts down and practice saying them out loud.

If your job requires you to speak under trying circumstances, or even if you just want to be able to say what is on your mind at a staff meeting, you need to plan to get good at this.

What can you do for better planning?

Be informed.

You can't do much planning if you don't know much about a topic. Learn all you can about the topics you might be expected to give an opinion on. Read your local newspaper and credible online resources. Read books (but be careful about reading just one book). Read magazines like Time and Maclean's that have some real content about the issues of the day. Talk to your manager, your colleagues, and your staff so you know their opinion or any expertise they bring to the table.

Don't make up your mind too early.

Keeping an open mind as you gather information is not easy, yet decisions we make in haste are ones that we often regret later. Try to keep analyzing the information as you get it. Is it accurate? Do you understand it? What can you do to be more informed?

Ask questions.

Don't assume that you have heard everything there is to hear, or that you understand a concept entirely the first time you hear it. Thoughtful people and critical thinkers will give themselves time to pause and reflect before commenting either positively or negatively on an idea. Asking questions and developing your listening skills in order to get all you can from the answers are two important communication skills to practice and develop.

Be aware of your own biases.

We all have some so they are nothing to be ashamed of. However, if we know what our biases are, we can keep them from influencing our decisions too strongly.

Weigh opinions against the facts.

Try not to be influenced by others' opinions until you have considered all of the facts. This is another way our biases can trip us up: you like a person so you give their opinion more weight than you should, or more weight than the facts (which may contradict that opinion). Or, conversely, you don't like a person so you disregard their opinion even when it is supported by facts.

Keep the information you gather organized.

Write down all the information you gather, or at least make notes about what you still want more information on. Identify the criteria you will use for evaluating the information. List the pros and cons, the costs and benefits, or use force field analysis (which we will discuss later).

Watch for traps.

Be aware of these ways your transfer of ideas can be confused, if you aren't prepared:

- **Derailment**: Somebody asks you a question and you lose your train of thought or head down another path, never to return to the path you originally were on.
- **Rocky Mountain Road**: Your presentation has no real theme or plan. You just lurch from point to

point. Neither you nor your audience is sure whether you will arrive at the end of your presentation.

- **Roller Coaster**: You make a good strong point, followed by a more obscure point, back to a strong point again, rather than starting with your best shot and working down to the details, or starting with the details and working up to your main point.
- **Whirlpool**: You say the same things over and over again, without getting anywhere or presenting new information.

Understanding Your Audience

For most internal presentations, you'll know the members of your audience or at least have heard something about them. You may also get asked to present to people that you've never met. Make sure you're informed in advance of everyone who may be coming to the presentation and do a little information gathering. This is your needs analysis, and will help you tailor your presentation in very meaningful ways, so don't skip it. Nothing is more unnerving than a walk-in appearance by the executive vice-president when you had planned an informal session with a few colleagues.

Once you know who the members of your audience are, start to construct a picture of them, either by asking yourself a few pertinent questions about them (if you know most of them and the subject is relatively simple) or by filling out an audience profile (if the group includes many people you don't know and the subject is relatively complex).

Filling out an audience profile form forces you to take the needs of your audience into account when you're developing your presentation. It may also alert you to a recycling point. That is, as you think about your audience and its attitudes, you may realize that your preliminary attempts to build consensus have been inadequate. If you discover that members of your projected audience are locked in apparently irreconcilable conflict, you may decide to defer your presentation until you have a better chance for success.

Write your objective at the very top of your audience profile and underline the action you hope to initiate. Then, answer the following questions:

- Who is the decision maker or decision makers?
- How much does the decision maker(s) know about the situation?
- How does the decision maker(s) view the situation?

- How will the decision maker(s) react to the proposal?
- Who else will attend the presentation?
- What are their views of the presentation or proposal?
- Who else will be affected by this presentation?
- What's the next step?
- What is my revised objective or fallback position?

Start your planning process in your listener's head. By determining what s/he needs, you will make it easier for her/him to understand you. In analyzing the audience's needs, also review their demographics, knowledge level and attitudes. These elements will be of assistance as you outline and flesh out your ideas.

Aim, Plan, and Convey

There should be three additional elements to your need's assessment:

Aim

Find a focus so that you make your information pertinent to your listener. Keep in mind not only what they need, but where they are coming from and how that will affect what they hear you saying.

Plan

Use a structured outline. Flesh it out with supporting evidence and visuals that reflect the listener's needs and agenda.

Convey

As you convey your message to your listener, watch for acceptance and make adjustments as needed.

Understanding Your Audience - Checklist Guide

What is my objective in making this presentation?	
Who is the decision maker or decision makers?	
How much does the decision maker(s) know about the situation?	
How does the decision maker(s) view the situation?	
How will the decision maker(s) react to the proposal?	
Who else will attend the presentation?	
What are their views of this proposal/point of view?	
Who else will be affected by this presentation?	
What's the next step?	
What is my revised objective or fallback position?	

Finding Common Ground

Listening for common ground and adapting your presentation or speech to it can be a powerful, persuasive tool. It can also help you defuse hostility and bring the group to your side.

Why?

Listening for common ground is a powerful intervention when group members are polarized. It validates the group's areas of disagreement and focuses the group on the areas where they agree with you.

Many disputes or issues contain elements of agreement. For example, civil rights activists often argue vehemently over priorities and tactics, even while they agree on broad goals. When disagreements cause the members of a group to take polarized positions, it becomes hard for people to recognize that they have anything in common with the speaker. This isolation can sometimes be overcome when the speaker validates both the differences between him/her and the group and the areas of common ground.

Listening for common ground is also a tool for instilling hope. People who believe they are opposed on every front may discover that they share a value, a belief, or a goal, and that will encourage them to participate.

How?

Listening for common ground is a four-step process. **First,** indicate that you are going to summarize where you and the group differ and where your concerns or issues are similar.

Second, summarize the differences. **Third**, note areas of common ground. **Last**, check for accuracy.

Here is an example:

- Step 1: "Let me summarize what I've heard you saying over the past few weeks. In some areas you think differently from me but in other areas, we think alike."
- Step 2: "It sounds like you believe… While I and my team believe…"
- Step 3: "Even so, we all seem to agree that…"
- Step 4: "Have I got it right?"

A variation is to **highlight an area of likely agreement**: "Several of you say this plan would cost too much. Do others think so?" Look around the room for signs of confirmation and if you see them, add something like, "Well, there is something you all agree on after all."

Overcoming Nervousness

Slight nervousness is normal for anyone, especially the first few times you make a presentation or speak in public. These jitters can actually help you and give you an edge when you take that nervous energy and deliberately use it as fuel for your presentation.

Nervousness has a way of spiraling, where you may notice all of a sudden that your heart is pounding, your knees are shaking, or your voice is trembling. Here are some helpful tips to get control back.

The **secret** you want to learn is not necessarily the confidence that comes from experience, although that helps, but a change in attitude. When you learn to shift your focus from yourself to the audience, you start to release the hold that fear has on you.

One of things that you will notice is that when you are well prepared for your presentation, you will feel less nervous about it.

While confidence can be built from repeated practice, a change in attitude also helps enormously. This requires that you shift your thinking from being all about you, to focusing on your audience. What are their needs? What is their agenda?

Nervousness can be attributed to many sources. These two are particularly important:

- One is the constant stream of **internal negative comments** that nags speakers when they begin to think about the presentation. ("I wonder how I'll come across this time? Last time I made a presentation, I was sure everyone was laughing at me when I had so much trouble with the equipment.")
- The other source of tension comes from **hyper-responsibility**. The presenter feels that he or she alone is responsible for the reactions and well-being of everyone in the room.

Think about it this way: you believe in what you're saying. You're prepared. In fact, for this presentation, you're the only person who is so well prepared. Your audience needs to know what you have to say.

Change the words you say to yourself from negative messages to more positive ones. List your concerns on a sheet of paper before the presentation. Then, for every negative message, substitute a positive one. For instance, if your negative message is, "I'm a nervous wreck," write, "I can channel this nervous energy into the presentation and give a more enthusiastic performance." This effort may take some repetitions, but if you give it a chance and believe in it, eventually it works.

Any tendency you have toward taking responsibility for everyone in the room can also be fought. Come to terms with the fact that everyone in the room will not necessarily accept your ideas. It's not your job to please everyone. **Your job** is to get your message across in clearly understandable terms to the people who must have the information. Concentrate on the decision maker and on those who respond positively to you. Ignore the others so that you can complete your presentation without their negative energy interfering.

It is hard to counteract nervousness if you do not feel in control of the situation, so take time before the presentation begins to put yourself in control.
Allow plenty of time to check out the room and equipment. Start on time. Unless the decision maker in your audience is delayed, don't wait for stragglers. Delaying will make you and your audience fidgety.
Greet people as they come in. Chat casually with people you know until it's time to start.

Eliminate any physical barriers that stand between the audience and you. If you're behind a table or lectern, move away from it. Don't cling to the podium or your projector. It makes you look nervous, and it really is a physical barrier between you and your audience. Removing barriers opens the way to meaningful conversation.

Sequencing Ideas

By putting your ideas into some kind of order, it will be easier for you to remember and easier for your listener to grasp your ideas.

- **Study**: Break your ideas into simple, basic components.
- **Separate**: Present each component separately.
- **Move Forward**: By building momentum successively with each component, you gain and keep your listener's interest.

This is another way of being prepared and controlling your jitters.

Controlling Physical Nervousness

- **Smile**. Look friendly and confident even if you don't feel that way. Your body will pick up on the positive energy and feelings that you generate, which will help you get centered.
- Take **deep breaths** to get oxygen into your brain.
- **Pretend**. There is never a better time to put on a false face of optimism and confidence.
- Your brain will respond to your positive self-talk, so **speak kindly** to yourself.

- Athletes **visualize** their entire event so that their brain and body can recall the feelings of success and help them perform well. When speaking, we can receive the same benefits from visualizing that athletes do.
- Expect to do well. Give yourself lots of **positive feedback**.
- **Remember** a time when you did well. Keep thinking of that time.
- **Speak about things you care about**, which will reduce jitters because your focus will be on the subject.
- **Avoid caffeine**, which can increase your nervousness.

Capitalizing on the Law of Attraction

We generally **get what we expect**. We can also create circumstances to get what we want. Positive expectations are one of the most powerful, outwardly identifiable characteristics that winning personalities demonstrate.

Evaluate your self-talk, the inner conversations you have with yourself. A winner's self-talk sounds like this: "I did well today. I'll do even better tomorrow." "I am getting to be a better speaker every day." A loser's self-talk is more apt to be, "Murphy's Law says whatever can go wrong will go wrong," or, "If I didn't have bad luck, I'd have no luck at all."

The **way you treat yourself** really shows in your results. If two people have equally rotten things going on in their lives (an earthquake or a tornado, for example), the positive person will recover more quickly than the negative one. Positive people live longer and are healthier than people who are negative.

Do you see where we are going with this? Embrace the **habits of positive, optimistic people** in order to develop those qualities within yourself, and you will find your fears of speaking in public much smaller than they ever were.

Dealing with Tough Situations

One of the reasons we are nervous is because we concentrate on us (the speaker) rather than other people (our audience). Putting the emphasis on the other person can help us forget about our own nervousness.

Sometimes we are the one responsible for a difficult situation. **How can we face the music ourselves?** We can learn how to apologize with grace and let other people know we regret what we said/did. Perhaps you got impatient, snapped at someone, or spoke rudely. An apology is in order.

One way to turn things around is to learn to **laugh at yourself**. It is not hard but it does take practice. If this is not something you will be still fretting about a year from now, it is not worth fretting about at all. Besides, we learn our most valuable lessons from our mistakes.

How to Make Your Listener Hear You

Use Nonverbal Communication

You're confident. You've rehearsed. You've got a powerful, logical argument. You're ready to take on the task of presenting your points in a way that does not distract from your argument. In management presentations, the drama should be in the content, not in the person. Once you're aware of the way people react to you, you can further refine the way you present yourself.

Leave the Appropriate Distance between You and the Audience

Although a public speaker may be 12 to 15 feet from the first row of listeners without being viewed as aloof and impersonal, a management presenter (who generally deals with far fewer people) should be no more than four to five feet away. If you're any farther away, the listeners may regard you as either stuffy or fearful. If you get any closer, people will become uncomfortable.

When you're speaking to a group with whom you have had little or no personal or professional relationship, start speaking from a position farther away and move in slightly as the presentation progresses and as you establish rapport. But don't get too close. A tall presenter, for example, who approaches within inches of his listeners and leans forward, is expressing dominance more than friendliness. To judge whether you tend to invade others' personal space, recall whether people ever inched away from you when you were engaged in informal conversations.

Physical distance rules vary from one culture to another. Some people often want to be within inches of each other when they speak, whereas others expect even more distance than you might be used to. Make sure that you know your audience.

Stand Tall

Good posture gives the impression of authority. You can correct poor posture by standing against a wall and pressing your spine flat against it. Feel what it is like to be standing straight, and make the most of it.

While you're making your presentation, make a conscious effort not to fold your arms. Folded arms seem to encourage slouching, and it certainly sends a message of defending or protecting yourself. There is a difference between good posture and stiffness, however. If you march briskly to the front of the room and do not move for the rest of the presentation, you signal rigidity more than authority.

Consider Your Appearance

A presentation is not the place to make a statement with your clothes – flashy clothes divert attention from your argument.

The standard business dress is suits with or without jacket and tie for men, although standards in non-traditional organizations may be more lenient, in general it is safer to stay on the side of conservatism. Anything too far from the norm or not appropriate for your target audience will cause the audience to fix on the distracting feature rather than your argument.

You want to convey competence in the subject matter, and what you wear can support you or undermine you.

Move About and Use Gestures

A presenter who stays glued to the overhead projector, the lectern, or any other one position is quite possibly terrified, and everyone soon knows it. To give the impression of self-confidence, move about the room and use your hands. Behaving like a confident presenter will help you to become more confident.

Take advantage of your natural gestures, but avoid using one over and over. Some presenters, when told that they need to add movement, adopt one gesture (raising an arm, for example) and use it repeatedly. At worst, such programmed gestures send the audience into a hypnotic state; at best, they're distracting. Tailor your gestures to reinforce your point. For instance, by bringing your hands together, you can assure your audience that your proposal "brings it all together." Similarly, you can refer to the ramifications of a problem by tracing ever-widening circles in the air.

Because most management presentations involve visual aids, you can add movement by simply pointing out the most important features on the visual. Moving around the room is helpful if it does not deteriorate into the measured pacing of a caged tiger. By pausing completely, you will emphasize the importance of what you are saying.

Control Your Facial Expressions and Mannerisms

Although we all know people who say, "If you cut off my hands, I wouldn't be able to talk," very few people actually overdo gestures. Facial expressions, on the other hand, are difficult to control and often give an embarrassingly accurate clue as to how you really feel. Beyond checking yourself on videotape, the best way to control facial expressions is to make sure you're comfortable with your material and prepared to respond honestly and openly to any questions.

Try to maintain an accessible, open presence. Remember that a smile breaks down barriers. When you smile at someone, they generally smile back. Also, as you talk, show interest in what you're saying. If you're not interested, how can your audience be?

Maintain Eye Contact

You will lose support faster by staring at your notes, looking only at the visual, or focusing on a spot high on the back wall than by any mistakes you may make in the content of your presentation. Similarly, if you direct yourself exclusively to the key decision maker in your audience, he or she will feel more uneasy than flattered, and others in the room will feel unimportant.

Try, at some point in the presentation, to look at each participant with the goal of giving each, in turn, the brief message, "I can see that you grasp what I'm saying." Then, for your own comfort, focus on people who respond with a nod or smile rather than on people who seem bored or hostile.

The Value of a Pause

If you are speaking within a negative or outright hostile situation, it is easy to become defensive and even angry. Instead of quickly answering every question (which increases the pressure and makes it difficult to maintain your composure), explore the value of a pause. A pause can give you a mini-break to collect your thoughts and deliver them well. It can also stop you from getting caught in an angry or emotional outburst.

Use pauses to your advantage. If someone asks a question and you need to collect your thoughts, you can take a moment to glance at your notes if you are using some, take a deep breath (not noticeable to anyone else), and then answer.

Connecting on Key Themes

By taking aim and finding a key theme, you will be able to focus your message specifically to your individual listener.

What is a key theme?

By putting yourself in your listeners' shoes, you can often find out what approach would make this topic understandable and interesting to them. When you make it as straightforward and simple as possible, you'll have a theme that holds their attention.

Why use a key theme?

- A key theme helps you plan.
- It also helps keep you on track.
- It leads your listener to your conclusion or recommendations.
- It holds your listener's attention and helps prevent boredom.
- Key themes help convey a memorable message. They also help your listener remember your message.

How do I find a key theme?

You may find your key theme by using experience from the past in dealing with this particular listener or common sense. When you defining your key theme, you can take a direct approach and ask a member of your future audience for their help. Discussing your topic with someone else can help you clearly articulate what you need to say.

Empathy is critical as you consider the needs of your audience. Your approach will be different (and your theme will be different) when you speak to teenagers about drinking and driving than it would be if you were speaking to Mothers Against Drunk Driving (MADD).

Key Sentences

After you have discovered and written down your key theme, take your virtual scissors and cut it down to key words: a 3 to 7-word sentence that will become your introduction (beginning) and conclusion (ending). This key sentence must be strong and impressionable.

Why use a key sentence?

- It is a short, direct statement that focuses you onto your key theme.
- It leaves your listener with a simple idea that keeps your message alive.
- It sums up your message with minimal distortion.

How do I write a key sentence?

- Talking straight and simply
- Using short, direct, familiar, concrete, single, short, words
- Creating pictures to hold the audience's attention
- Keeping adjectives and adverbs to a minimum
- Using active tense, not passive
- Keeping it simple and avoiding clutter

Remember: Stop, Think, Plan, React

- Scan the situation
- Decide on your objective
- Create your plan
- Keep your eye on the objective

How to Structure Ideas

We have already been working on a three-part plan: opening, body, and closing for every presentation or response we make. However, now we are going to zero in on the body of your plan, to make your message as persuasive as possible.

Remember, the essence of Speaking Under Pressure is quick and structured thinking which allows you to persuade your listener. What you want is a memorable message conveyed quickly and clearly. You have defined your strategy and done some preparation work. You are now ready to create planned approaches and to practice some new skills.

You only need to harness 3 key points

We recommend that you outline three key points for the body of your presentation. Your introduction (beginning) and conclusion (ending) will be short additions to your key points. Let's talk about why we recommend three key parts.

Aim

In order to send a memorable message, you must aim your presentation in a logical and organized manner. You want to leave no doubt in your listener's mind what you are trying to say. He/she must be able to catch the essence of your presentation. So, let's stick to facts, ideas, and points of view that are best suited to your particular listener.

You want your listeners to catch the softball aimed at them. They should not have to duck out of the way of a muddy message. Having only three points will help you create a clear target for your presentation.

Make sure you have already found out what your audience wants to hear and figure out how you can give them at least some of what they want. Try to speak in clear, easy to understand words and sentences. We don't trust people we don't understand.

Concentrate

You must have a plan in order for you to concentrate on clear thinking. The stronger your sense of organization, the less likely you will become confused or hampered by emotions and personal opinions.
By using your pre-programmed plan, keeping it simple and direct, you make your point clearly. If your thoughts have been well organized, they will be clear and easy to present.

This means that you can give your full attention to getting your message across and looking and sounding confident and sincere as you watch your audience.

Adapt

You must have a good grasp of the purpose of your presentation so that you are free to scan the situation repeatedly; to read and to react to your listener's needs and wishes. By having a plan, you will be free to adjust to and explain ideas which are aimed at your individual listener's needs.

Adapt when necessary. Watch for agreement: eye contact, a smile, a nod of the head. Watch for confusion: a wrinkled brow, a quizzical expression. Watch for disagreement: a scowl, folded arms, inattention. Then you can react as required. Get feedback. Add examples. Allow questions.

Depth

We learned that planning helps to cure jitters and that planning is simple. Planning involves the orderly sequence of ideas (study, separate, move forward). In order to create some depth to the study, there must be enough components or parts.

Two points are too few, yet five or six might be too many for people to consider at one time. Three or four points work best because they are simple, yet offer opportunity for analysis.

Move Forward

We noted that it is important to have a dynamic presentation, one that moves along. Three points offer enough components to create a sense of motion; perhaps even a sense of anticipation.

Ease

Three points are easy to remember; therefore, easy to present and convey.

Your 3 Part Plan Template

My Key Theme

_____

_____

_____

Opening

_____

_____

_____

Body – Point One

Body – Point Two

Body – Point Three

Closing

_____

_____

_____

_____

Get Organized Using Time, Place and Aspect

Experienced presenters and speakers often use file cards or sticky notes when they collect information, since they can be easily arranged and rearranged. By arranging them in piles, you can create an organizational plan and add or delete information without the need to redo the entire presentation. There are also software programs that enable this kind of simple reorganizing.

Here are the steps to organizing your information.

1. Write only one point on each card or sticky note.
2. Arrange the cards into piles, putting all closely related points together. For example, all evidence related to economic development goes in one pile, all evidence related to profiling the community goes in another pile, and so on.
3. Arrange the piles in one of the following basic ways:
   - **Time**: Organize information from past to present to future. The time plan is easy to picture (clock, day/night, etc.) and to create. Use of past, present, future can often help make sense out of any jumble of facts, especially when you have little time to prepare.
   - **Place**: Everyone can visualize a map or globe as you travel with your listener from place to place. The place plan lends itself to topics which are geographically separated. Remember to leave the most important place

for last for maximum impact. You may want to create forward motion by arranging items in geographical direction.

- **Aspect, factor, or focus**: Examining the topic from different perspectives. Visualize an equidistant triangle. You examine the key theme from three different points. You will find this plan especially helpful in serious situations when you want to create the impression of being fair-minded.

- **Problem-analysis-solution**: Description of the problem, why it exists, and what to do about it.

- **Order of importance**: From least important to most important, or from most important to least important.

- The choice of sequence will depend largely on the logic of the subject matter and the needs of your audience.

4. Go through each pile and arrange the cards or sticky notes in an understandable sequence within your basic plan. Which points need to precede others in order to present a clear picture?

5. Write out your organization plan to create an outline. Use it as your road map while you write your message.

Two Additional Methods

The methods we just discussed are the most common ways of organizing material before you present it. However, there are many other options. Here are two examples.

Zoom Lens

You may start with a specific example and then move to a more general perspective, such as from one fisher to the whole industry. (This is called the **divergent approach**.) The reverse can also work: moving from a general perspective to a specific example. (This is called the **convergent approach**.)

Pendulum Plan

This examines the issues in terms of **extremes**, such as no businesses open on Sunday to every business open on Sunday, and then settles on a **mid-point** where some businesses are open on Sunday. This can be difficult to do successfully yet it can also be a very effective way of demonstrating your ability to compromise or to seek a middle ground.

The Meaning Behind Your Message

While our words deliver a significant message, our non-verbal signals also provide their own message. You know that you are in sync when the two are working together!

In significant (though often misinterpreted) research, **Albert Mehrabian** found that when it came to discussing emotions, only 7% of the speaker's message was communicated by words, and that tone of voice was responsible for about 38% of the meaning and body language about 55%. This means that the words themselves played only a very small part in conveying meaning. In other conversations (not the ones about emotions), we know that tone of voice and body language have a large impact on what we are saying.

The face and the eyes are the most expressive means of body communication. Additional positive or negative messages are sent by your gestures, posture, and the space between you and the other person. Body language must be in tune with your words and tone or you send a mixed and often confusing message. Positive body language is important to supporting your words and ensuring complete understanding.

Remember, your attitude is projected through your voice as well as your body language. Make sure your body language always says, "I know what I'm doing and saying," or, "I'm here to help as best I can."

The speed or rhythm of your speech is important as well. Clear communication includes appropriate pauses and inflections to support your words.

Qualities of a Good Voice

- **Alert**: Awake and interested
- **Pleasant**: A smile in your voice (when appropriate)
- **Natural**: Straightforward language, without jargon
- **Enthusiastic**: Glad to speak
- **Distinct**: Easy to understand with moderate volume and rate
- **Expressive**: Well-modulated, varied tone

Remember:
- Have a clear message
- Have a theme or key word for each point

- Create depth (points sufficiently different to be noticeable, yet still tied together)
- Create movement (advancing your case for a certain conclusion)

Beginnings and Endings

Some **general points** about beginnings and endings:

- You really do only get one chance to make a first impression, so make it good and make it count. If you lose their attention at the beginning, it's really hard to get it back. Make things easier on yourself with a good hook.

- The beginning and ending must be coherent with the content of your message; they must add to the unity of the overall presentation.

- The beginning and ending should be a brief indication of what is to come and a summary of what has been. You don't have to build in a surprise.

- The duties of the beginning and ending are to highlight your key theme, send out a mental picture of where you are going, and to make the plan move forward.

There are three purposes to a good beginning:

- **Orient** your listener to your key theme. State it directly and indicate exactly what it is you are going to talk about.

- Provide them with a sense of **direction** by summarizing your outline in the beginning.

- **Hint** to your listener what your conclusion will be.

An ending should:
- Summarize what you have just said.

- Finish by restating your key theme. You want to reinforce your message and leave your key theme as a residual element that listeners will continue to think about.

When writing an ending, you should:
- **Stop**: Pause. Take a moment to reflect on your message.
- **Think**: Study, compartmentalize, and analyze to ensure you are seeing things from the audience's point of view.
- **Plan**: Review your outline and then prepare an ending that wraps up your message. Consider whether you also need to tell them what their next steps are.
- **React**: Respond to your listener, audience, or customer to give them what's needed.

Delivering Your Message

Often, it is not so much what you say as how you say it. Let us look at some ways that you can deliver a clear, effective message.

Use direct language and deliver a message that is clear, calm, and direct. Be confident in your message. This means that your tone of voice, vocabulary, and rate of speech convey your feelings. Be careful not to back down (at least not immediately) if you are discussing something that is important to you. Be considerate of other people's ideas, but do not quickly give up on yours, especially when you have it all well thought out.

Factual descriptions and relevant details are more likely to be heard. Look at this generalization: Joe never gets his work finished. Compare it to something specific: Joe has not met his goals for an entire month.

Use **repetition** respectfully and to keep things on track. Conversations can easily get off track, especially if they get emotional or if someone is trying to steer the conversation away from what you felt was important. Do not be afraid to restate your purpose during an interaction.

Be as aware of your **non-verbal messages** as you are about your verbal messages. Also consider other people's communication style: are they direct or indirect? Passive or assertive? Make sure to also take into account their filters, assumptions, and beliefs. This will help you to keep your message clear.

Do not include words with hidden meaning that can be misleading or not plainly understood. Do not use jargon or acronyms that are unfamiliar to your audience and that will leave some people feeling left out. If terms are known only to people who work within your industry or in your company, either do not use them at all, or explain what they are before using them. Do not make the assumption that everyone will know what they mean, even if they do work within your industry or your company.

What are some aspects of your message that can be pared down? Keep only relevant information in your message.

Often less is more. Readers want information the fastest way they can get it, and this means conveying the information in a simple, fast and effective way. But remember to include important details such as the 5Ws: Who, What, Where, When, Why.

Check for Understanding

You do not have to wait for the end of a conversation to make sure you and your conversation partner understand each other. You can check for understanding throughout the conversation to make sure that things are on track by using some of the following questions or statements.

- What do you think about what I just said?
- Let us summarize what we have covered so far.
- Please tell me what you are thinking.
- Does that make sense?
- If you were going to share this with the team, what would you say?
- What is not making sense here?

Great ways to add meaning to your message include:

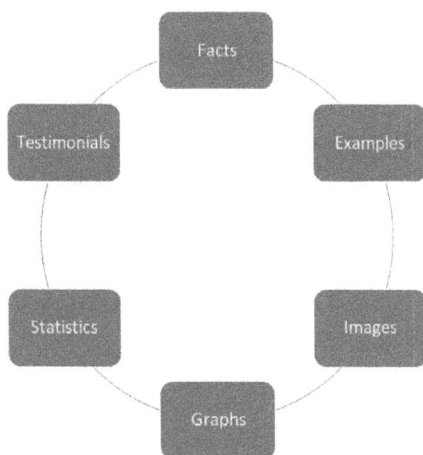

Can your message be expressed differently? This could include the use of a song, a music video, or a Ted talk video of an expert. There are so many ways that you can hone your message without reinventing the wheel. If someone already has a great message that you are trying to share, use it to get your message across.

Expanding a Basic Plan

So far, we've concentrated most of our efforts on very short, two-minute responses, because these are the opportunities to speak that most often come our way and that we want to use to our advantage. Generally, longer presentations are not spontaneous. You've been forewarned of longer presentations, so you have time to prepare.

However, you may want to take what we've discussed and use those ideas to make a longer presentation. This session will give you some ideas on how to fatten up your basic plan by filling in the subsections and reinforcing your argument. In this process, you can include evidence that supports your key theme. The results of your audience analysis should allow you to pick examples and illustrations at the listener's knowledge level which will clarify your points. The listener's attitudes will also influence what evidence you use to prove your points.

Some techniques that can help you build on your basic plan are listed below.

Symbols

Use fat words that paint pictures, rather than thin words that leave no impression on our minds. Find the most striking circumstances involved with whatever you are describing. A well-chosen example can be so powerful that it becomes the focus for the point being illustrated.

Opposites

Compare and contrast. Getting a solid idea of similarities and differences can make decision making easier. For example, if you are debating what kind of coffee to have in the office, you can compare fair trade with open market coffee by assessing their similarities. If you wish to provide contrast, you have to assess the differences between two things.

Statistics

Statistics can be rounded off or made specific. When rounded off, they are easier for the audience to remember. When they are more specific, the audience gives the stats more credibility but may have difficulty remembering the figures. What method will best work for your audience, give you credibility, and be remembered?

Tips and Tricks

Be sure that any extra content **strengthens** your conclusion or recommendations.

You can **vary the type of plan you use** to create interest and maintain your listener's attention. If your boss has heard your short presentation once or twice and has invited a few guests in to hear your full idea, remember that you have to keep him engaged as well. This can be especially important when they are considering several presentations and will select what projects will get priority, for example.

You can **vary the number of subsections** to create movement. Review but don't restate too often or you run the risk of becoming boring. Sometimes we get into a rhythm where we put a new slide up, say five sentences, and move onto the next slide. Mix it up and be memorable. Your presentation needs to focus on your message, not the number of slides you can pack together.

People love stories, and a story helps us to remember the point, as long as it is memorable and connected to your presentation. Resist the temptation to use other people's stories and look at your own. See if you can adapt it to fit your point, and add some variety and/or meaning to your presentation.

Evaluation Template

Speaker:

	Yes	No	Notes
Theme for message			
Theme for points			
Depth			
Movement			

Beginning strong			
Ending summarized			
Illustrative devices			
Speaker poised and confident			
Sounded sincere, credible, knowledgeable			
Convinced me			

"Let your dreams be bigger than your fears"

CHAPTER 4

COMMUNICATE WITH CONFIDENCE

"They may forget what you said, but they will never forget how you made them feel" – Carl W. Buechner

D o you get nervous when presenting at company meetings? Do you find it hard to make conversation at gatherings and social events? Do you lock up in awkward social situations? If so, this course and chapter in particular are for you!

We'll give you the confidence and the skills to interact with others, to speak in informal situations, and to present in front of small groups.

How do we get to be better communicators? To make powerful, impressive, and lasting presentations, start from within.

- **Talk to yourself.** Clarify the message in your own mind before you try communicating it to someone else.

- **Rehearse**. Nothing clarifies your thoughts more than writing them down, and then saying them in different ways until you get them to where you want.

- Be very aware of the messages or **inner tapes** you are playing to yourself. Don't sabotage yourself by giving yourself negative messages about your ability to communicate, or about how the other person will take your message.

- Most of us are way too hard on ourselves. Plan what you will say and then **be optimistic** that it will come out right and be received well.

- Who is stopping you from being **self-confident** and **self-reliant** right now? I'm not stopping you. Have a look at any barriers you are putting up and make a decision to deal with them.

- When you speak to individuals, take the time to express yourself in an **organized** manner. Don't rush.

- **Clarify**. Ask for feedback. Do not assume that the message sent was the message received.

- Take part in all the activities we'll be doing today. When you take part, you are preparing yourself to **be a leader**, rather than a follower, in your workplace and your community. You are being a role model for your colleagues, your children, and those who look up to you in other ways.

- Know when to **stop talking**.

When presenting to a group, make sure you:
- Have a message worth communicating
- Understand your audience and what their needs are
- Gain the listener's attention
- Emphasize understanding
- Get feedback
- Watch your emotional tone
- Persuade them to adopt your point of view or take the action you want them to take

Today you will have several opportunities to practice the skills of speaking in public. Use these exercises because they are good learning opportunities and practice makes perfect.

Barriers to Communication

Listening

The two most basic elements of good communication are listening to others and asking questions. The physical process of **hearing**, where sound enters your eardrum and is registered in your brain, is not the same as listening. **Listening** is more of an attitude, a desire to understand what is being communicated. It is an essential communication skill.

Many of us don't listen very well, and we fake it a lot of the time. We pretend we are listening when we really aren't, and that can create a whole lot of trouble with other people.

The good news is that we can all learn to be better listeners. We can talk about listening in terms of two types of listening:

- **Passive Listening**: We hear the sounds but we aren't taking an attitude that allows us to hear the message.
- **Active Listening**: We make a conscious effort to hear and understand the message.

Steps to Active Listening

- Non-verbal cues, such as eye contact, leaning toward the speaker, and an alert expression on your face.
- Short verbal cues, such as "Uh-huh," "Yes," "I understand," etc.
- Feedback: Where the listener summarizes, clarifies, or asks questions.

Getting ready to listen means becoming prepared psychologically. It is like thinking, "OK, another person is taking a turn and I must get ready to listen." It is important in a group that every member finds a useful way to listen.

When we make a decision to listen for total meaning, we listen for the **content** of what is being said as well as the **attitude** behind what is being said. Is the speaker happy, angry, excited, sad, or something else entirely?

Responding to Feelings

The content (the words spoken) is one thing, but the way that people feel really gives full value to the message. Responding to the speaker's feelings adds an extra dimension of listening. Are they disgusted and angry or in love and excited? Perhaps they are ambivalent! These are all feelings that you can reply to in your part of the conversation.

Why Don't People Listen?

Let's take a look at the problems and some possible solutions.

The listener has decided in advance that the speaker or the subject will be uninteresting.
This leads the listener to tune out. Instead, tell yourself you will make a real effort to learn something new during the conversation and put effort into listening.

The listener is distracted when someone is speaking.
Choose an area without distractions. Refuse to be distracted.

The listener didn't adjust to what the speaker was saying. For example, you were talking about the weather, but the topic has now shifted to what the speaker did on vacation.
This requires some mental agility. You could ask the speaker to slow down and give you time to shift gears.

The listener took too many notes.
Rather than copy down every word, just note key points. This takes practice, but is worthwhile mastering.

The listener felt that what was being said was too difficult to understand so they tuned out.
The listener should ask questions to clarify, or ask the speaker to illustrate the point. The speaker can also watch for non-verbal cues that the listener is getting confused and adapt their language to help communication.

The listener got sidetracked by their own biases.
Let's say the speaker used the word "refugee" to refer to the people made homeless by a flood or earthquake. You prefer the word "victim." This may be important to you, but try not to raise this point until the speaker has had opportunity to complete their thoughts.

The listener jumped in too soon to relate their own ideas or experience.
Be patient. Listen. Give the other person their turn. Then present your ideas or experiences, if appropriate.

The listener listened only for the facts and didn't pay attention to body language.

This is all about increasing your awareness of those around you and how they are reacting emotionally to what is being said. Learn more about body language to help you.

The listener was daydreaming.
Self-discipline is required to listen. Bring yourself back to the conversation by internally saying "stop." Remember to make eye contact to connect with the speaker. This will also help you to stay engaged.

Asking Questions

Get in the habit of asking good questions to clarify what has been said. We can do this by paraphrasing ("Are you saying…?") or by asking other questions such as, "Do you mean…?"

Other open questions that can gather more information include:

- What do you think we can do about this?
- What would you like me to stop doing?
- Would it be helpful if I…?
- Supposing we were to…?
- Help me understand where you're coming from?
- Let's set a time when we can talk about the changes, we're both prepared to make.
- I'm prepared to… Would that help with the situation?

Think about three people that you consider to be good listeners?

What is Said and What is Heard

Some people seem to be naturally good communicators, while others have to work at it. Communication skills are not related to how bright we are, either; people can be gifted in their subject matter, but struggle with communicating what they know or to connect with people.

What we say isn't always what the other person hears. Our message goes through a complicated system of filters and outside influences before it reaches the recipient. We must always clarify that the person has received the message that we intended to send.

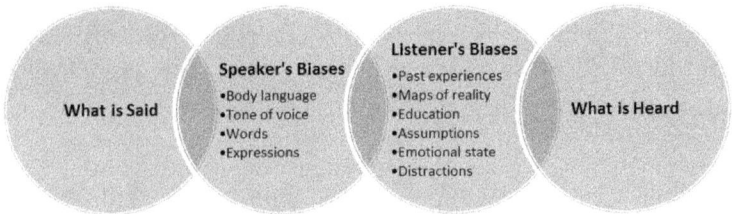

How Do You Rate Your Listening Ability?

One reason listening is so important is that we do so much of it every day. We often say that good communicators spend far more of their time listening than they do talking. Fortunately, listening is a skill that we can develop. In an age when we are inundated with media messages and portable devices, we can choose to listen more than many people seem to be.

Listening Assessment

Answer the questions on the test below. Don't answer the questions too quickly; it is easy to confuse what you know is right from what you actually do.

Question	Yes	No	Points
Do you enjoy listening?			
Is it easy for you to listen with interest to a large variety of subjects?			
Do your friends seek you out to discuss a problem or decision when they need help?			
Does your attention usually stray toward other groups or people entering or leaving the room?			
Do you interrupt?			
Are you more apt to be thinking ahead to what you will say next rather than weighing what you are being told?			
Do you stop listening to everything when you strongly disagree with the speaker on one point?			

Do you assume or anticipate regarding the other person's views?			
Do you feel you can judge most people quite quickly before hearing them out?			
Do you generalize (All old people think... all redheads... all college kids...)?			
Do you encourage others to elaborate or clarify points you have misunderstood?			
Do you listen to what is not said, such as the obvious omission?			
GRAND TOTAL			

Scoring

Give yourself 2 points if you answered "Yes" for question 1. You enjoy listening as much as you enjoy talking.

Give yourself 2 points if you answered "No" to questions 4, 5, 6, 7, 8, 9, and 10.

Give yourself 2 points if you answered "Yes" to questions 2, 3, 11, and 12.

Your score: _____

Interpretation

If your score is **20 or more**, you've already developed some strong communication skills. You have the ability to listen to people, understand what they are saying, and communicate your understanding back to them. Use your listening and communication skills to help others.

If your score is between **10 and 18**, you're within the average range. Use this quiz to help you identify where you're doing well and where you would like to do better.

If your score is **less than 10**, it's time to start learning! Use this quiz to help you set some goals. Start with one or two things that you would like to improve on, such as empathizing, paraphrasing, or asking good questions. Then, we'll work on setting an action plan, and you'll be on the road to being a better listener, and a better communicator.

Active Listening Skills

The problem is that listening and hearing are not the same thing. Most of us were fortunate to be born with hearing, but listening is a skill that must be learned and practiced in order to use it successfully. When you **hear** something, sound enters your eardrum, passes through your ear canal, and registers in your brain. **Listening** is what you do with that sound and how you interpret it.

Here are some tips for successful listening:
- Listen intentionally for people's names.
- Listen with interest.

- Try to get rid of your assumptions.
- Listen for what isn't said.

Listening is hard work. When other people are listening to us, they have the same difficulties we do in trying to focus on a message. Our minds wander, noises or thoughts distract us, and we can be thinking about what to do next.

Active listening means that we try to understand things from the speaker's point of view. It includes letting the speaker know that we are listening and that we have understood what was said. This is not the same as **hearing**, which is a physical process, where sound enters the eardrum and messages are passed to the brain. Active listening can be described as an attitude that leads to listening for shared understanding.

When we make a decision to listen for total meaning, we listen for the content of what is being said as well as the attitude behind what is being said. Is the speaker happy, angry, excited, sad…or something else entirely?

Responding to Feelings

The content (the words spoken) is one thing, but the way that people feel really gives full value to the message. Responding to the speaker's feelings adds an extra dimension of listening. Are they disgusted and angry or in love and excited? Perhaps they are ambivalent! These are all feelings that you can reply to in your part of the conversation.

Reading Cues

Really listening means that we are also very conscious of the non-verbal aspects of the conversation.

- What are the speaker's facial expressions, hand gestures, and posture telling us?
- Is their voice loud or shaky?
- Are they stressing certain points?
- Are they mumbling or having difficulty finding the words they want to say?

Demonstration Cues

When you are listening to someone, these techniques will show a speaker that you are paying attention, providing you are genuine in using them.

Physical indicators include making eye contact, nodding your head from time to time, and leaning into the conversation.

You can also give **verbal cues** or use phrases such as "Uh-huh," "Go on," "Really!" and, "Then what?"

You can use **questions** for clarification or **summarizing statements**. Examples:
"Do you mean they were charging $7.00 for just a cup of coffee?"
"So, after you got a cab, got to the store, and found the right sales clerk, what happened then?"

Tips for Becoming a Better Listener

- **Make a decision to listen.** Close your mind to clutter and noise and look at the person speaking with you. Give them your undivided attention.

- **Don't interrupt** people. Make it a habit to let them finish what they are saying. Respect that they have thoughts they are processing and speaking about, and wait to ask questions or make comments until they have finished.

- Keep your **eyes** focused on the speaker and your **ears** tuned to their voice. Don't let your eyes wander around the room, just in case your attention does too.

- Carry a **notebook** or start a conversation file on your computer. Write down all the discussions that you have in a day. Capture the subject, who spoke more (were you listening or doing a lot of the talking?), what you learned in the discussion, as well as the who, what, when, where, why, and how aspects of it. Once you have conducted this exercise 8-10 times, you will be able to see what level your listening skills are currently at.

- Ask a few **questions** throughout the conversation. When you ask, people will know that you are listening to then, and that you are interested in what they have to say. Your ability to summarize and paraphrase will also demonstrate that you heard them.

- When you demonstrate good listening skills, they tend to be **infectious**. If you want people to communicate well at work, you have to set a high example.

Getting Comfortable in Conversation

Four Levels

Being comfortable speaking with others in small social settings can have a big impact on both your personal and your professional life. We are all more drawn to the person who looks at ease and confident than we are the person who looks ill-at-ease and awkward. Individuals who can carry on a conversation have stronger relationships. They also tend to be more confident when it comes to speaking in public.

At work, our first encounter with another person often begins with a handshake and a smile, while looking directly at the other person. This does not include staring at another person unblinkingly, but rather, looking at their face: the eyes, nose, and mouth triangle.

Level One: Small Talk

What can you do to give yourself an advantage when striking up a conversation? Let's spend a little bit of time talking about the different levels on which we communicate.

Small talk means a very superficial conversation about the weather, the traffic, current events, etc. While this may seem purposeless, it isn't. This is our chance to size up another person and decide whether you have something in common. You don't know the other person and you aren't expected to reveal anything personal about yourself.

We are aware of a young teenager who had a hard time in conversation with people her own age (especially boys!). She decided that since lots of the boys she knew were interested in sports, it would be a good idea to learn about some of the sports they enjoyed, and to be able to talk about them.

Not only did she manage to attract lots of new friends, she also found out how much she enjoyed sports at the same time. This technique was something that she shared with her girlfriends. Taking an interest in other people and the things they are passionate about is a great way to get into a conversation.

Level Two: Fact Disclosure

When the small talk phase goes well, we are ready to move onto the second level of communication with our conversational partner. We will reveal a few facts about ourselves, such as our occupation, our hobbies, or the types of activities we enjoy.

Now that you are revealing a bit more about yourselves you may find more you have in common. There is give and take in this conversation as you ask and answer questions with your partner.

Level Three: Viewpoints and Opinions

Generally, people don't move to this stage until they feel comfortable with one another and believe they have found common ground when you disclosed facts in the second level. In this level you go beyond that to give your opinion of whatever it is you've been talking about.

Examples:
- Skiing is an expensive hobby

- Your dream is to ski in Jasper, Alberta
- You are counting the days to retirement
- You are hoping to move to another job soon

You may even venture into such quagmires as politics or religion if you are feeling comfortable enough to do that. The general rule is "low and slow," as in don't reveal too much too soon.

You may want to commiserate about the high cost of sending a child to university today, but wait until you know the person better before you reveal that you took out a second mortgage to send your child to university.

Level Four: Personal Feelings

This usually doesn't come until you feel very comfortable with your conversational partner. The surest way to get here is to not reveal too much too soon. An example of too much too soon might be telling someone all the details of a messy divorce just five minutes into meeting them, or upon learning someone is of a different political party, launching into a condemnation of that party.

A successful conversation starts at level one and proceeds at a comfortable pace through the second and third levels and continues to the fourth level, although usually not during your first meeting. With some people, you will find yourself moving easily through at least the first three stages, if not to stage four.

It usually takes a lot of conversations with someone you feel very comfortable with before you progress to level four.

Professionalism

Looking Professional

The way you look really does say a lot about you. Dressing professionally will help you be more confident when you speak, so dress the way you want to be perceived. Look like you care about what you are doing.

Always appear as **neat and clean** as possible, with hair and fingernails that are clean and neatly trimmed, and shoes that are clean and polished.

Choose your clothes carefully so that you look **trim** and **neat**. Be sure clothing fits properly. You won't feel good and you won't look good if your clothes are too tight. If they are too loose, you may look like you don't care. Dress comfortably and be proud of who you are.

You don't have to dress like a fashion maven, nor spend a lot of money trying to keep up appearances. If you are building your wardrobe, consider consignment and second-hand resources, which can be an excellent way to build a wardrobe on a **budget**. Make sure that you learn the colors and styles that suit you and stick to them.

No matter what we want to believe, **your clothes matter**. You will feel much more confident if you dress up than if you dress down. **Just try it and see what happens!**

It is also very important to dress appropriately for the audience and the occasion in order to gain their trust and attention quicker and break through any pre-judging mind-sets quickly.

Maximizing Meetings

Four Areas of Opportunity

Meetings are a central part of communication and cooperation within any organization. Don't think of them as drudgery. Recognize them as opportunities to develop skills and develop your reputation, as well as a chance to stay on top of essential organizational information.

Anticipate.

If you receive an agenda ahead of time, take a few minutes to look it over. If you see areas where you may have an opportunity to take the lead or to provide information to others, use that opportunity. If there is no agenda, ask for one.

Prepare.

Do your homework. If you plan to speak on an issue, know what you are talking about. Keep your comments positive and speak with enthusiasm. The direct, relaxed approach works best. Get quickly to your point and stay with it. If you are raising an issue of complaint or concern, it will be better received along if you include reasonable solutions. Busy people have little patience with more than they want to know. However, clarity and conciseness take preparation.

Participate.

- When should you speak up?
- When you know you can clarify a point?

- When you can supplement pertinent information or furnish convincing statistics
- When you can correct an error
- When you wish to ask a question
- When you can give credit that's due
- When you have a good idea or an original suggestion
- When someone else has taken your idea and presents it as their own

Be brave! A great way to get more confident at speaking in front of others is to volunteer to chair meetings. Let your boss know that you want to improve and that you are up to the challenge!

Concentrate on Your Message

What does the audience need to hear? Focusing on your message and your audience instead of your nervousness will help to boost your confidence. Put the power in your message instead of holding onto it and giving you a case of nerves to deal with.

Public speaking is an opportunity for you to share what you have learned, broaden your network, and consider how the impact that you want to have can be shared.

Whether you are pitching an idea, managing a crisis, or leading a meeting, effective speaking skills are critical to building credibility and carrying your message home. Even the most secure speakers know that they shouldn't wing it. No matter how well you know your product or service, or the story that you will share, it pays to plan. Think about what's most relevant to your audience and put their interests first.

The numbers of people who aren't good speakers far outweigh those who are good, so there's lots of room for those who are just okay at public speaking. However, if you want to move your presentation from dull to dynamic, you can pump up your presentation in seven easy steps:

1. **Talk to yourself.** Practice in front of a mirror, trying to look relaxed and friendly. Stand with your arms in front of your body, with your elbows at 90 degrees and your palms at 45 degrees, leaning forward. That says, "I'm here, I'm engaged, and I am being open with you."

2. **Have a point.** Decide on your core message ahead of time. Bring the listener quickly to the point of action by crafting your theme into your introductory passages.

3. **Look them in the eye.** Making frequent eye contact for a few seconds with listeners in the audience will create an aura of confidence and familiarity, which will help you get your message through. This also helps with making an emotional connection.

4. **Know the room.** Boost your comfort level by checking out your speaking venue in advance. Practice with the microphone and any visual aids that you plan to use.

5. **Crack a smile.** Smiling tells the audience you're enthusiastic and confident – just the kind of person they want to hear.

Smiling can also relax you, reduce your heart rate, and help you breathe easier.

6. **Pump up the volume.** People need more energy than they think to make a strong presentation. Use a slightly louder voice than you think you need, and work on your articulation.

7. **Don't be a comic.** When you tell a joke, you can easily offend other people. Tell a funny story about yourself instead. And write your own material – nothing damages credibility more than telling someone else's story and pretending that it is yours.

8. In order to be remembered as an effective presenter, it helps if you become very good at **remembering names**. A lot of people say they are terrible with names. That usually means they have not taken the time to master the art of learning people's names.

Preparing for Meetings

Our weeks are often filled with meetings. They are an excellent forum for sharing information and knowing what's going on, if they are managed well. Otherwise, meetings can seem like a big waste of time. To make the most of your meetings, we have several tips for you.

Before the Meeting

You need to be one of those people who are prepared for meetings when you arrive. This means arriving on time, reading materials that are supposed to be reviewed beforehand, and being prepared to participate as opposed to observing.

- Questions to ask yourself when preparing for a meeting include:
- What information do you need to take with you?
- What do you want to get out of the meeting? Is there something in particular you want to get done?
- What contribution do you want to make?
    - Are you just trying to get information?
    - Do you want to follow up something that was raised at an earlier meeting and check progress on it?
    - Do you just want to draw attention to something?
    - Do you want to make sure people are aware of a problem so that it doesn't happen again?

When previewing reports and information, here are some tips:

- When the reports arrive, scan them quickly to establish the scope and content.

- Write down any initial questions you may have and look for answers in the subsequent stages.

- Read conclusions, summaries, and recommendations first, then go back and read the content. (This improves retention of the material.)

- Highlight sections or use sticky notes to make sections you want to refer to.

During the Meeting

Keep your contributions short.

Your point is more likely to be understood and to have an impact if you keep it reasonably short. Resist the urge to go off on a tangent.

Don't take so many notes that you lose track of what is going on.

Most meetings are recorded by a minute-taker, so just write down the things that affect you (such as things that you are responsible for doing before the next meeting) or things that will jog your memory when it comes to reporting back to your employees or supervisor.

Avoid interrupting others to make your contribution. Do not let others interrupt you.

In some meetings it is difficult to get your contribution in. If you do have to interrupt, do so firmly and politely. Once speaking, do not be tempted to make several points for fear of not getting in again.

Think about your non-verbal behavior.

Both the volume and tone of your voice are important here. If you are too quiet you will lose impact and be open to interruptions. Eye contact is also important. Remember to sit somewhere that makes it easy to catch the eye of the chair so that you can get your contribution in. While you are speaking, distribute your eye contact throughout the meeting, but direct it at those for whom your contribution is most relevant. This enables you to judge how your contribution is being received.

Time your contributions.

Raise points at the relevant time for the maximum impact. Do not wait until the last minute before airing an opposing view. If others are on the verge of making a decision, they will be irritated if you suddenly come up with opposition.

If you are brief and avoid interruptions, you stand a good chance of getting a reaction. If no one reacts, however, don't be shy about asking the group or an individual for a reaction.

If you are asked to give an opinion on something that has come up unexpectedly, don't feel pressured into giving an off-the-cuff answer if you are not confident that you know your own strengths. It is perfectly acceptable to ask to be given time to think about it.

Leading Meetings

If you are leading meetings, here are five ingredients for managing them effectively:

Be a leader or member of the meeting committed to resolving issues, not just talking about them.

Hold meetings that focus on important issues and guide the group in resolving them.

Make sure that meeting leaders and members have the skills needed to work together effectively.

Establish a means for recording ideas and keeping track of what goes on.

Arrange a meeting location free of interruption from other activities.

CHAPTER 5

SELF DISCOVERY AND SELF CHECK

"It usually takes me more than three weeks to prepare a good impromptu speech" – Mark Twain

Speaking Characteristics

Self-confidence is an important element of public speaking. We grow our confidence when we are able to master one-on-one conversations. Then we can more easily make the transition to developing our presentation skills.

The characteristics below can make or break the audience's impression of a speaker. These are things you may not give a lot of thought to, but members of your audience will. Taking control of them can make you a dynamic and well-respected speaker.

Volume

Play with your volume and get control of it. Varying volume allows you to emphasize by being louder or softer at times. Get a good idea of your natural volume: too loud is hard on listeners, but so is too soft. Listen to people who deliver the news or who act as commentators. They use variety for maximum effect.

Clichés

When we are not sure what to say, we all fall back on old sayings. What makes them into clichés is that overuse makes them less interesting and tired. The most interesting speakers try to avoid saying things the same way everybody else does. Instead of saying the baby's skin is, "Soft as a feather" we might say, "Soft as…" or instead of saying, "As hard as nails" we could say, "As hard as…"

Diction

Diction is about the way you pronounce and enunciate words. If you do not know how to pronounce a word, look in the dictionary or ask somebody who knows the correct pronunciation.

Make an effort to speak clearly. While you want to sound natural in your presentations, most of us need to slow down and be more precise so that everyone can hear what is being said. Mumbling makes it difficult for the other person to know what we have said. If you know you chew your words, or otherwise make it difficult for people to understand you, start practicing and developing better speaking habits.
One excellent resource is to join a Toastmaster's chapter or another speaking organization. There are chapters around the world and there is vast benefit from the time you would invest.

Slang or Vulgarities

You may feel more comfortable when you are with friends and slip into local sayings or swearing. You might work in an organization where this is the norm, too. However, when you are presenting, it is important to project a professional image. Remember that you have a message to share and maybe people to convince. Do not undermine your own credibility by losing sight of what you need to do.

Gender References

In order to be inclusive in what you say, you must be sensitive to both masculine and feminine terms for example, nurses are not always female and doctors are not always male.

Think about how you can speak in terms of non-gender specific?

Acronyms and Jargon

If terms are known only to people who work within your industry or in your company, either do not use them at all, or explain what they are and then use them. Do not make the assumption that everyone will know what they mean, even if they do work within your industry or your company. Assume no knowledge and make it easy for people to follow along with by avoiding acronyms or explaining them as you go.

Tact

Tact means making full use of diplomacy. This means saying the right thing at the right time, but also leaving the wrong thing unsaid.

Benjamin Disraeli, explaining his popularity with Queen Victoria said, "I never deny. I never contradict. I sometimes forget."

How often do you avoid other people because they always seem to say the wrong thing? They express themselves in such a way that it hurts or offends you or others. These people lack tact. Tact is a demonstration of skill and grace in dealing with others. It means that how you say something is as important as what you say. Tact enables you to maintain good interpersonal relations by not offending others.

Five Golden Rules

Here are five rules to remember in order to have better conversations.

1. Talk to yourself in positive terms. Take time to clarify the message in your own mind before you try communicating it to someone else.
2. When you speak to individuals, take the time to express yourself in an organized manner. Use a pause to gather your thoughts.
3. Ask for feedback. Do not assume that the message sent was the message received.
4. When presenting to a group, have a message worth communicating.
5. **Know when to stop talking.**

What Is Your Type and How About Mine?

The Assessment

There are many ways to describe personality types, with the idea that there are base temperaments that we can relate to, and that we prefer. The science behind this kind of assessment relates back to the work of Carl Jung, which was later advanced by Katharine Cook Briggs and her daughter Isabel Briggs Myers.

Identifying Your Characteristics and Preferences

We have developed an assessment that can help you identify what your base temperament is. First, look at the group of words. For each group, decide which of the four choices is most like you, a lot like you, somewhat like you, and least like you. It is important to answer the questions according to what feels right, and not what you think people think about you or may expect.

First, select the one that is most like you and write the number 4 on the line. Then select the term that is a lot like you and write number 3 on the line. Then write number 2, and then 1. You must use the numbers 4, 3, 2, and 1 in each section. There are no ties allowed, so you need to make a decision on each group. You can see an example on the next page.

Remember that you are working on preferences and not a math exam, so do not get overly tied up in absolute definitions!

When you are finished the questionnaire, follow the instructions on the scoring sheet.

Example
Scale

- 4 = Most like you
- 3 = A lot like you
- 2 = Somewhat like you
- 1 = Least like you

Terms

1. A driving need for you is:

3	C	To find meaning in life
4	A	To learn and gain knowledge
2	B	To belong
1	D	Freedom to do what you want

Questionnaire

1. A driving need for you is:

C	To find meaning in life
A	To learn and gain knowledge
B	To belong
D	Freedom to do what you want

2. A primary need for you is:

D	Making an impact
A	Maintaining calm
C	Relationships
B	Responsibility and duty

3. Which of these things interests you?

C	People
A	Ideas
B	Information
D	Actions

4. You respect:

	B	Authority
	A	Intellect
	D	Performance
	C	Relationships

5. You:

	C	Stick up for what you believe
	D	Are constantly busy
	A	Look to the future
	B	Like to provide for others

6. You like:

	A	Exploring
	B	Security
	C	Cooperation
	D	Seizing opportunities

7. You are good at:

☐	D	Making quick decisions
☐	B	Looking after details
☐	C	Inspiring others
☐	A	Solving complicated problems

8. You want:

☐	D	Variety
☐	A	Logic
☐	C	Harmony
☐	B	Stability

9. You prefer to focus on:

☐	B	Structure
☐	C	Relationships
☐	D	Action
☐	A	Knowledge

10. You value:

	D	Action
	B	Security
	C	Self-improvement
	A	Intelligence

11. You make decisions by relying on:

	C	Intuition
	D	Senses
	A	Data
	B	Tradition

12. You enjoy:

	D	Adventure
	B	Social gatherings
	C	Meaningful interactions
	A	Theories and data

13. Your work stressors are:

☐	D	Inefficiency
☐	C	Boredom
☐	B	Injustice
☐	A	Not knowing

14. You appreciate:

☐	C	Skilled performance
☐	A	Research and investigation
☐	B	Cooperative interaction
☐	D	Respect for policy and tradition

15. Your leadership style is

☐	D	Firm, fair, respectful
☐	C	Relaxed, flexible, open
☐	B	Patient, supportive, encouraging
☐	A	Logical, inspirational, direct

Scoring

Add the total number of points that you wrote beside each letter of the alphabet in the questionnaire. Pay close attention, since the letters above are not always in order!

Example

In our sample at the beginning of the questionnaire, we would add 4 points to the A column, 2 points to the B column, 3 points to the C column, and 1 to the D column.

A	I I I I
B	I I
C	I I I
D	I

Your Score

A	
B	
C	
D	

Total A's _____ Total B's _____ Total C's _____ Total D's _____

The letter with the highest total is most like you. Write it here:

_____

The other letters are your next preferred styles. If your numbers are close to each other (within five points), you probably find it fairly easy to flex your style to those other categories. If your numbers are far apart, or one is much lower than the others, that is the area you will find it challenging to work within. You will have the knowledge of how to do it once you work through the material below.

What Does it Mean to Have a Number?

In reality, we are a blend of all types, moving within the numbers and flexing into the other styles that our circumstances and our comfort levels dictate. This means that we are more like a blended drink than distinct ingredients. You will recognize that you may behave one way at work (super organized), usually be more relaxed at home, but return to your super organized self when stress at home increases. As you read the descriptions below, see if they agree with how you behave as a presenter. You will also gain some insight into how to connect with the different types in the descriptions.

Mostly A's – Inquiring Rationales

Inquiring Rationales are often **drawn to jobs such as banking and engineering**. They like to figure out how things work. They consider the structure and configuration of things. They process information intuitively and look at the big picture. These are visionaries, such as Albert Einstein and Bill Gates. When it is time to make decisions, they apply logic, and they do not get persuaded by emotions. If they do not respect you, you will not keep their attention. Experience and competency are very important to Inquiring Rationales.

This temperament profile makes up approximately **five to seven per cent of the population**. Other notables in this group are Walt Disney, Ben Franklin, Margaret Thatcher, and Napoleon.

To connect with Inquiring Rationales in your audience, demonstrate your expertise in your introduction and opening. Quote experts and remember to cite your sources. Get to the point – and your content – quickly. Broad statements are acceptable only if you can back them up, so be certain to have your statistics and data ready. To keep their attention, use facts and figures first and personal stories later.

If this is your preferred speaking style, your strength will be in the architecture of your speech. Your ideas are founded in the science, not hyperbole. Your presentation will be logical and creative, and you will even back up your own theories with evidence. To keep things moving, do not be afraid to add some stories and quotes to the mix.

Your weakness as a presenter or speaker is predictability. Too much logic might mean that you are giving a presentation that only other Inquiring Rationales can understand. Learn how to incorporate humor and make your presentation interactive. Use stories to add depth and warmth; other people will thank you for it! Avoid staying glued to your PowerPoint slides and remember to step away from the podium to engage your audience.

Mostly B's – Authentic Idealists

Authentic Idealists are **natural teachers, counselors, and leaders**. They are benevolent and intuitive, and they focus on global issues like world poverty and humanitarian issues. Idealists love metaphors, stories, and symbols, rather than statistics and figures. They make decisions that reflect their values, and rely on emotion and instinct as opposed to logic. In fact, statistics and facts bore them. They are looking for significance, and they seek the truth.

The Authentic Idealist temperament makes up about **10 per cent of the population**. Notable members of this group include Eleanor Roosevelt, Billy Graham, Mahatma Gandhi, Jane Goodall, Oprah Winfrey, and Albert Schweitzer.

To connect with the Authentic Idealists in your presentations, share your values and personal convictions. Be authentic and reach out to them by telling stories that demonstrate your empathy. Appeal to personal ethics and a higher calling. Show that you care about them and each person in the room. Authentic Idealists are more interested in how much you care than how much you can cite statistics.

If your speaking style is that of an Authentic Idealist, your strengths include making deep connections with your audience at an emotional level. You are a good storyteller, so find innovative ways to present your information. You have wisdom to share and are eager to do so. Your lack of ego about what you know makes you likeable.

If you have a weakness, it is your sensitivity to the audience. You are intuitive and will interpret meaning behind everything. This also means that you can get distracted by reactions of individuals in the audience, and that can make you lose track.

Your speeches tend to be powerful but can lack humor and get too emotional. You may also tend to believe that speaking from the heart is all you need, and you may not plan your presentation very well. You might be tempted to wing it. Make sure that you do not.

Mostly C's - Organized Guardians

Organized Guardians are extremely **dependable and loyal**, and they play by the rules. They have an amazing work ethic, stay down-to-earth, and they like routine. They are thorough and orderly. At times they are too serious, but they are practically always serious. They are good at taking care of other people. They want to hear about the bottom line, and they want the facts. They can often be your hardest and most judgmental members of the audience.

Organized Guardians will consider charts and graphs and will follow a well-prepared presentation longer than most people. They can shut down when too much emotion is presented and may get bored with stories. This temperament makes up **40 to 45 per cent of the population** and includes people such as Queen Elizabeth II, Mother Teresa, George Washington, and Colin Powell. With their respect for tradition, they are drawn to the military and policing. These are also the people who will pass traditions to their children and grandchildren.

To connect with Organized Guardians in your audience, be concise, organized, and support statements with data. Present information in logical sequence and do not wander off down a tangent. Quote other experts.

If you are an Organized Guardian as a speaker, you will be very logical and organized. You will probably use PowerPoint because that is what people use, and you will have slides with plenty of bullets and numbers. Make sure you do not have more slides than you absolutely need!

Your weakness as a speaker can be predictability and a dry speech. The data will be there, but not the heart. You may have far more material than you need because you think it is all important. This means that your speeches can be too dense and without humor. Draw on your compassion for others to add emotional depth to your presentation.

Mostly D's – Resourceful Artisans

Resourceful Artisans **crave action and live in the moment**. They are very social, confident, and persuasive. Steven Spielberg and Madonna are notable Resourceful Artisans. They are witty, playful, and fun. If they had a message to share, it would be that the world could lighten up a little. They love playing to an audience and look at the world as their stage. Like Organized Guardians, they can also perceive the world concretely. They can get bored with visionary tasks. They enjoy stories that they can easily relate to and imagine happening to them. This temperament makes up about **35 per cent of the population**.

To connect with Resourceful Artisans in your audience, be real and spontaneous. Do not stand behind a podium and read off your notes or slides. Engage them with questions and discussion. Use well-developed, engaging personal stories and let your creativity show. This style wants you to deliver an experience, not just a speech.

If you are a Resourceful Artisan as a speaker, your strengths include energy, personality, and creativity. You will deliver a show. You will get a thrill from the emotional connection between you and the audience. Build in some interaction to leverage your spontaneity. You are a natural storyteller, so tell some stories.

Your weakness might be in your organization and structure. Because you are living in the moment, you will avoid the homework that goes into the development of a brilliant presentation. You might avoid preparation and be willing to rely on spontaneity. Be careful not to be so spontaneous that you miss a good opportunity to deliver a message. Have fun, but stay on track.

What's Important About This?

We all have preferences for how we do things, and now we hopefully understand a bit more about them. It is also important to remember that we ALL have the range of temperaments described here.

We just have our own preferences; you might be mostly A, but call on behaviors that are more closely associated with B, C, or D as needed.

When making presentations, keep in mind your personality type as well as the fact that your audience will likely contain a range of types.

Positive Self-Talk

Our Thoughts

To make powerful, impressive, and lasting presentations, we have to start inside. What kinds of things are you telling yourself? There is a factor that affects our ability to speak with or to others 100 per cent of the time: **OUR THOUGHTS!** Our thoughts create feelings, our feelings lead us to choices and action, and the action we take (or do not take) produces our results.

If you see all your faults and recite them to yourself when you look in the mirror, your self-esteem takes a regular beating. If you look in the mirror and say to yourself, "I like my hair today," or "I have a friendly looking face," your self-esteem grows a little bit and you become more confident of your ability to do things such as speaking in public.

Listen to your inner voice and the self-talk you give yourself. If you can hear the negative messages, start replacing them with new, objective, positive self-statements. You can build your self-esteem and be much more confident when you are talking to others. You can put the emphasis on them rather than on you.

The 4 Steps to Feeling Good

Emotion	Describe the Events that Triggered this Emotion	What Kind of Thoughts Lead to this Emotion?	How to Replace the Negative Thoughts
Sadness or depression	*Example: Events that involve a loss: a romantic rejection, the death of a loved one, job or money problems, aging, poor health, the failure to reach a personal goal.*	*Example: You may tell yourself you can never be happy without the thing you have lost, or that person whom you loved so much. You may feel a loss of self-esteem because you tell yourself you are inferior or unlovable.*	*Example: Identify that this is only one aspect of your life.* *Identify ways that you can minimize the sense of loss.*

121

Guilt or shame			
Frustration			
Anger			
Anxiety, worry, fear, panic			
Loneliness			
Hopelessness or discouragemen t			

Building Rapport

We develop rapport with people so that we can communicate openly and with trust. If our presentations are intended to persuade and convince someone to do something, we have to establish trust with our audience, and that is not a quick or easy task. Equally, if you are presenting to people you do not know well, you will not trust them either.
A sense of belonging and connectedness is a deep need we all have.

One way to make these connections is to have an introduction that explains who you are, what you do, and why you are doing the presentation. Depending on the nature of the presentation, you will also benefit from some self-disclosure in that introduction: a nugget that aims to connect to something in common with your audience.

Whether you are presenting to a crowd of 100 or there are just three people in the boss's office, that introduction says a lot.

Body Language Signals

A significant amount of someone's message is conveyed through their facial expressions and body language. What do you know about body language? What does the other person's body language say to you?

Poker players try to mask their body language and hide any signals that will tell their competitors what kind of hand they have. Psychologists teach their students how to read subtle signals that can show on your face when you try to hide the truth, mask a surprise, or you are nervous. Our best piece of advice is to **make your face look friendly**. Smile, or at the very least be aware of whether your face is tense and angry looking. If so, purposely relax your facial muscles and turn your lips up at the corners. You look more approachable that way.

While we have probably all heard that **crossing your arms** makes others feel you are not listening to them, or that you have a closed mind, we know that is not always true. Sometimes your cross your arms because you are cold, you cannot think of anything to do with your hands, or you spilled soup on your tie. Whatever the reason, it tends to send a negative message to others. If you often cross your arms, try to break that habit.

One of the most important things you can do with body language **is learn how to identify cues from people that indicate you are making them uncomfortable.**

If you sensitize yourself to these simple cues, over time, people will have the experience of feeling more relaxed, at ease, and open with you. In any case, they are quite simple, but most people do not pay enough attention to them. The most common signs that someone is becoming uncomfortable are:

- Rocking
- Leg swinging
- Tapping

These are the first sign of tension and indicate that the person feels intruded upon or nervous. If it escalates, these signals are often followed by:

Intermittent closing of the eyes

Slight tucking of the chin into the chest
Shoulder hunching
Basically, learn to watch for these signals, and then adjust your approach when you see them. Sometimes just taking one step back gives people the space they need. Asking questions instead of talking (thereby getting the other person to talk to you instead) can be all it takes to ease the tension and re-engage someone.

I Can Just Send an E-mail, Right?

Are you ever tempted to skip a meeting or conversation with a hope that you can replace the contact with a note instead? It is so easy to send an e-mail, or call early in the morning and leave a nice long message, especially if you would rather not make a presentation. But wait! Did you know that **oral presentations are generally more persuasive than written ones**?

Researchers have tested the way the brain responds to stimulation through language, visual images, and music. They have found that the spoken word engages both the right (creative, intuitive) and left (analytical, logical) sides of the brain.

Written material appeals more specifically to the analytical side of a person's brain This means that, since most people make decisions based on both rational and intuitive criteria, you are more likely to gain acceptance for your proposal through an oral presentation. This method appeals to both sides of the brain, as opposed to a written report, which appeals to only one side.

Besides, **part of persuading involves getting to know people**. Since you are here to improve your presentation skills, let's focus on building those relationships by getting there in person rather than taking the easier route.

Given the sterile nature of asking for something you want in written form, when you meet with people in person you can add some **energy, enthusiasm, and passion**. You can add more information if they have questions, check their body language, and work with it. Rarely can the enthusiasm communicated in a phone call or a meeting be duplicated in a letter, e-mail, or memo.

Mastering Non-verbal Communication

You are confident. You have rehearsed. You have a powerful, logical argument. You are ready now to take on the task of presenting your points in such a way that you do not distract from your argument. In management presentations, the drama should be in the content, not in the person. Once you are aware of the way people react to you, you can control the way you present yourself.

Leave the Appropriate Distance between You and the Audience

Although a **public speaker** may be 12 to 15 feet from the first row of listeners without being viewed as aloof and impersonal, a **management presenter** (who generally deals with far fewer people) should be no more than four to five feet away. If you are any farther away, the listeners may regard you as either stuffy or fearful. If you get any closer, people will become uncomfortable.

When you are speaking to a group with whom you have had little or no personal or professional relationship, start speaking from a position farther away and move in slightly as the presentation progresses and as you establish rapport. But do not get too close. A tall presenter, for example, who approaches within inches of his listeners and leans forward, is expressing dominance more than friendliness.

To judge whether you tend to invade others' personal space, recall whether people ever inched away from you when you were engaged in informal conversations.

Physical distance rules vary from one culture to another. Some people want to be within inches of each other when they speak, whereas others need much more space. Be aware of where you are and what is expected.

Stand Erect

Good posture gives the impression of authority. You can correct poor posture without difficulty by standing against a wall and pressing your spine flat against it. While you are making your presentation, make a conscious effort **not to fold your arms**. Folded arms seem to encourage slouching, and it certainly sends a message of defending or protecting yourself.

There is a difference between good posture and stiffness, however. If you march briskly to the front of the room and do not move for the rest of the presentation, you signal rigidity more than authority.

Consider Your Appearance

A presentation is not the place to make a statement with your clothes – flashy clothes can divert attention from your argument. Be professional and choose clothes that suit you.

Although standards in non-traditional organizations may be more lenient, in general, it is safer to stay on the conservative side. Anything too far from the norm will cause the audience to fix on the distracting feature rather than your argument.

Move About and Use Gestures

A presenter who stays glued to the overhead projector, the lectern, or any other one position is terrified, and everyone soon knows it. To give the impression of **self-confidence**, move about the room and use your hands. You may even convince yourself that all is well.

Take advantage of your **natural gestures**, but avoid using one over and over, and try not to be conducting an orchestra. Some presenters, when told that they need to add movement, adopt one gesture (raising an arm, for example) and use it repeatedly. At worst, such programmed gestures send the audience into a hypnotic state; at best, they are distracting.

Tailor your gestures to reinforce your point. For instance, by bringing your hands together, you can assure your audience that your proposal "brings it all together." Similarly, you can refer to the ramifications of a problem by tracing ever-widening circles in the air.

Because many presentations involve visual aids, you can add movement by simply pointing out the most important features on the visual. **Moving** around the room is helpful if it does not deteriorate into the measured pacing of a caged tiger. By **pausing** completely, you emphasize to your listeners the importance of what you are saying.

Control Your Facial Expressions and Mannerisms

Although we all know people who say, "If you cut off my hands, I would not be able to talk," very few people actually overdo **gestures**. **Facial expressions**, on the other hand, are difficult to control and often give an embarrassingly accurate clue as to how you really feel. Beyond checking yourself on videotape, the best way to control facial expressions is to make sure you are comfortable with your material and prepared to respond honestly and openly to any questions.

Try to maintain an **accessible, open presence**. Remember that a **smile** breaks down barriers. When you smile at someone, they generally smile back. Also, as you talk, show interest in what you are saying. If you are not interested, how can your audience be?

Maintain Eye Contact

You will lose support faster by staring at your notes, looking only at the visual, or focusing on a spot high on the back wall than by any mistakes you may make in the content of your presentation. Similarly, if you direct yourself exclusively to the key decision maker in your audience, they will feel more uneasy than flattered, and others in the room will feel unimportant.

Try, at some point in the presentation, to look at each participant with the goal of giving each, in turn, the brief message, "I can see that you grasp what I am saying." Then, for your own comfort, focus on people who respond with a nod or smile rather than on people who seem bored or hostile.

Using Notes

It is hard to imagine anyone trying to memorize a presentation word-for-word. Recall takes so much energy that you would have little left for relating to the audience. Do not ever consider memorizing. Instead, learn to use notes **unobtrusively** and **effectively**.

Many presenters use their **visuals** as notes. If your visuals are not sufficient to remind you of the details, you can construct notes in several forms. However, you do it, your notes should be easy to use. In terms of **content**, you should include your opening remarks as well as your ending remarks and any statistical information that is too difficult to remember and will not appear on your visuals.

For **long presentations**, your notes may go into more detail than is necessary for short ones. If you plan to use extensive notes, underline key points or use a highlighter. In either case, however, never use full sentences because you may lapse into reading them and thus destroy your phrasing.

Two popular note-taking devices are to write simple key words or phrases on index cards or on the frames of your PowerPoint notes.

Index Cards

Never walk around holding your index cards or notes. Let them remain on the lectern or the table so that you are free to make assertive gestures without waving your notes around.

PowerPoint Notes

Simply add notes in the provided area when creating your slides, and then print them off to use during your presentation.

When you are using PowerPoint, try not to be mesmerized by the words and graphics on your screen. Also, do not read from the slides – use them to illustrate your points and keep you on track.

Managing the Question-and-Answer Period

Just as you sometimes encourage questions during your presentation, be sure to **invite participation when you are finished**. Say something simple like, "I will be glad to answer any questions you have." In some cases, you may want to ask people you know to pose one or two questions just to get the discussion going.

Regard this portion of the presentation as a chance to:

- Gather new information
- Stress your main point
- Get commitment to your plan of action

No matter how well you have prepared, someone in this group may have information you do not, or may contribute something you have not thought of. Your **ultimate goal** is to contribute to the success of your organization. Questions, comments, and discussion serve that goal very well. The more people who participate and the more questions they ask, the more effective you are likely to be.

The first step in **responding to questions** is to listen very carefully. Nod to show that you are paying attention. Do not be surprised if the question has to do with a point you are sure you covered in your presentation. You may not have put your point across as clearly as you thought. Other members of the audience invariably identify with the questioner, not the speaker. To say, "Well, I thought I covered that in my remarks," or to sigh resignedly and roll your eyes, cuts off discussion and damages your credibility with the audience.

The following **guidelines** should also help.
- Establish ground rules
- Let people finish
- Respond to everything, even statements
- Restate the question
- Stay on track
- Admit you do not know the answer
- Control the discussion
- Move toward action

➢ Practice and Practice out load
➢ Time yourself – presenters that run over time put pressure on the conference event organizer so make sure you run to time and keep an eye on timing as you proceed
➢ Wear something that can take a microphone lapel and battery pack easily
➢ Use images on slides to provoke your thought rather than slides of dot points. If you use dot points keep it to a minimum of 3-5 per slide
➢ Don't clutter slides with your text
➢ Avoid detailed charts and graphs that the audience will not be able to read
➢ Include video if possible

- Include some quiz like or thought-provoking questions as you proceed to foster engagement and attention
- Have some back up slides after the closing slide if you need to use them to extend your talk
- As a guide for a 30-minute talk – 20 slides would be the maximum.

Believe in yourself and your message and be excited for the opportunity to share your message
Think of the audience in terms of a group of friends or students you are teaching rather than an overwhelming crowd.

1. Subtly sell or refer to your services do not hard sell during your presentation. Confidence in knowledge and expertise sells your products better than you pushing them. People that have bought tickets to learn something and conference organizers that need to attract the audience get turned off if they feel they are just being sold too rather than being educated.

2. Ensure you promote yourself across your social platforms as a speaker at the conference

3. Think about what you want to share afterwards to delegates and have it ready to go. Conference organizers need to turn this information around quickly to delegates to ensure they have enjoyed the full experience with exceptional service – it may be some summary points rather than your entire presentation deck which you may want to protect for IP reasons but also slide decks are to prompt your own discussion points and often do not mean much to the delegates when they look at them on their own post the event i.e. they need your voice to obtain the detail of your presentation.

4. Think about an offer or a download link you might like to extend delegates in order to assist you in capturing leads, what value can you give them that also allows you to follow up and make contact post the event.

5. Watch the video replay – this is how you learn and improve your presentation skills

6. Share conference photos post the event and thank the organizer, also add the speaking event to you CV or website.

The Five S's for Presentation Success

It can be hard to remember to cover all of the bases for any presentation, particularly if you are put on the spot. The five S approach will work for any size presentation. If you are put on the spot in the lunchroom, you can use this approach to provide a quick, complete answer. If you are giving a large presentation at a conference, you can use this approach as a framework. Either way, it will ensure that you tell the audience what they want to know and what they need to know.

The framework looks like this:

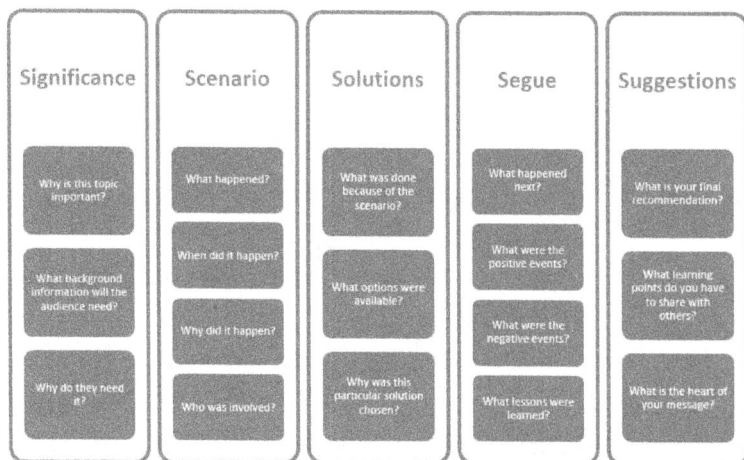

Significance	Scenario	Solutions	Segue	Suggestions
Why is this topic important?	What happened?	What was done because of the scenario?	What happened next?	What is your final recommendation?
What background information will the audience need?	When did it happen?	What options were available?	What were the positive events?	What learning points do you have to share with others?
Why do they need it?	Why did it happen?	Why was this particular solution chosen?	What were the negative events?	What is the heart of your message?
	Who was involved?		What lessons were learned?	

Example

I was drowning in clutter: too many clothes in my closet, too many books on my bookshelves, and too many pieces of furniture in my house. I did not have time for a yard sale. Besides, we live on a pretty quiet street without much traffic. However, I needed to get rid of things and I could not bring myself to throw them out.

So, I bagged and boxed all the items I no longer wanted and I called a local charity. They came by with a truck and took everything away. They made money, I felt good, and my house was de-cluttered. If your possessions are starting to take over your life, I recommend calling This Charity at 000-0000.

Evidence

Sometimes you will be presenting evidence to your audience. Perhaps you want to convince your audience that cats should be on leashes if they are outside their own backyard, or you want to convince your boss that you deserve a promotion. Whatever you are trying to prove and whomever you are trying to persuade, you can help your case if you have solid evidence that will impress your audience, and if you have arranged those arguments in the most logical order.

This does not mean there is only one way to present your information. It does mean taking some time to gather your evidence and then taking a few extra minutes to organize it into the most effective argument you possibly can.

Evidence involves **answering the following questions**:

What will convince my audience? Depending on the people in your audience, some want statistics and facts first, and others will connect to the emotion of your appeal.

Which is the best order for this situation?

Bring along any evidence that will support the claim you are making. Graphs, charts, photos, reports, and even models will all give your presentation that added punch.

Introductions

Your introduction should:
- Grab their attention
- State your purpose
- Explain your agenda
- Show personal and specific benefits

Other ways to begin your presentations include:
- A question asking about the audience's concerns. This can be an effective beginning in a small group. The drawback to this approach is that it commits you to considering all the topics your listeners may bring up. In other words, use this technique only when you know the issues the audience will raise and are prepared to discuss them all.
- A rhetorical question, such as: "Can you teach people to be creative?" A rhetorical question is meant to be thought-provoking. It must be carefully crafted for this purpose. In doing this, ensure you do not inadvertently make a snide suggestion that you know something the audience does not – not a good way to build rapport.
- A statement of your qualifications. If no one has presented your qualifications, and especially if the group is hostile, this approach can help you establish rapport.

Following the Opening Statement

If, in your opening statement, you have not told the audience what the presentation is about and why it is important, do so next. Keep in mind that an audience will remember best what you say first and what you say last. Do not waste the first few moments.

Beginnings and **endings** are critical because audiences are most alert during the first minutes and final minutes of a presentation.

Your beginning must tell:
- **What** the presentation is about.
- **Why** the subject is important.
- **How** you will develop the argument.

If you have chosen not to share criteria important to the audience in the body of the presentation, you must deal with them in the beginning.

Transitioning to the Body

If you are concerned about your rapport with members of the audience, work to build their confidence by stating your criteria or responding to theirs.

You can make a natural transition into the body of the presentation by concluding the beginning with guidelines for how you will proceed. These are called **signposts**. They make your thoughts an easy trail to follow.

Example

Is there anyone in this room who would not like to earn more money? **(This is my attention grabber!)**

Tonight, I am going to bring you three easy, sure-fire strategies for being more successful at your job. None of them are difficult. I have used all of them and I can tell you from personal experience that they work. In fact, I went from working as a $14 an hour call-center operator to a six-figure salary in just two years using the techniques I will describe to you tonight.

Furthermore, I will give you specific, step-by-step instructions for using each strategy. You can take your own notes if you wish, but some of us are not that great at note-taking, so I have included every word in this CD that you can buy at the end of the program for just $7.98. **(This is your beginning.)**

My first strategy is to get very comfortable speaking in public. **(I have given you a signpost. This is my first point. Now I am ready to launch into the body of my speech.)**

Enhancing Your Presentation with Stories, Numbers, and Examples

No matter how brilliantly you speak, your audience will remember your points better when they are supported with appropriate pictures and stories.

However, while most people agree that stories and examples are one of the most effective devices in a memorable presentation, they can also be the most difficult for speakers who struggle with spontaneity. If you have done a bit of preparation and you have some examples, it will help you add this punch without worrying about being creative on the spot. This is another place where your audience analysis will really pay off.

Endings

An effective ending repeats the recommendation (or in this case, the strategies that were presented) and reinforces the need for action.

Continuing with the **previous example**, my ending would summarize these points:

- Become more comfortable speaking in public. Take a course, join Toastmasters International, or just offer to speak at every service club in your area, free of charge. I do not care what you have to do. Get out there and make yourself known.

- Spend some money on a fashion consultant so you look good. That will not mean spending tons of money on clothes but it will mean spending your money on clothes that flatter you, not clothes that are necessarily trendy.

- Create a website that establishes you as a speaker. Use your own name and choose a small list of topics that you are knowledgeable about.

Then, you want to **end on a strong point**: something that will keep them thinking and propel them to act.

Closer for this example: Get out there and earn YOUR money!

Your Speaking Voice

Parts of Your Message

Tone

Tone refers to the way that you distinguish or inflect your words. We use tone to express emotion, emphasis, contrast, and other features of our speech. Your tone tells your audience **how you are feeling about the words you say**. Good intonation lets others see your attitude and your enthusiasm for your subject, and demonstrates that they are consistent.

Which do you prefer: monotonous or melodious? Do your words come out pleasant and energetic, or lifeless and wooden? Think in terms of friendliness and a desire to communicate with others and develop the best intonation that you can to captivate listeners to what you have to say.

Pitch

This refers to how high or low your voice is. In most cases a **low-pitched** voice is considered an asset. Men and women who have lower voices are considered more exciting, more credible, more sociable, and more relaxed. They are also generally easier to hear when you are in the audience. If you have a **high-pitched** voice, be aware of it and consider how you can best deliver your message. If you have a high voice and will speak frequently, working with a vocal coach can be an excellent idea.

Pacing

This refers not just to the speed at which you speak, but also the length of the pauses in your speech. The ability to pace your speech and use your voice to create impact is the single most important skill you need. For example, **which pace is more effective**?

Bad management costs jobs.

Bad…management…costs…jobs.

Emphasis

You can dramatically change the **significance of what you say** in a presentation by stressing words which would normally be unstressed or contracted. As an example, change the meaning of the simple question "Who am I?" by stressing a different word each time you say it.

Which is more dramatic?

"It is not cost-effective."

"It is NOT cost-effective."

You can also make your statement more **persuasive** by using simple intensifiers (such as "just") to emphasize your points. As an example, "I am afraid it just is not good enough. We need the entire system overhauled."

Facial Expressions

Our face is an **extremely expressive part of our body**. The facial expressions you use when you talk are important because they create a distinct impression about you. If you have too much tension in your facial muscles you may appear to be angry or uptight. Keep your eyes open, your brow unfurrowed, and an alert and animated look on your face if you want others to perceive you positively.

Eye Contact

Most people do not realize what a negative and alienating effect poor eye contact can have on their total image. Good eye contact does not mean staring into another person's eyes and not breaking contact. This can make people feel as uncomfortable as not looking at them at all. Good eye contact means looking in the **general vicinity** of the person's eyes, watching the whole face, and occasionally making direct eye contact. It is about making that person feel like he is the only person in the room. When you are making a presentation, do not look over people's heads to the back of the room. Rather, look at individuals around the room, spending five to 10 seconds with each of them.

Posture

Your posture is one of the first things people look at, and they do use it when they make judgments. Your posture is the key to communicating your image. You do not want to come across as either too stiff or too sloppy. Stand straight, as though you are an important person. Hold your head high.

Body Language

Body language is a broad subject, incorporating eye contact and the range of non-verbal cues. However, here is a summary of some common body language that can send negative or positive messages.

Positives	Negatives
Open body language	Tapping your fingers or feet
Sweeping gestures	Arms crossed
Palms up	Glancing at watch
Leaning forward	Leaning back
Natural, smooth hand gestures	Tense body

Vocal Variety

Below are some well-known sayings. Go around the room so everyone has an opportunity to try saying one of the phrases with as much vocal variety as possible.

- Luck is what happens when preparation meets opportunity.
- The easier it is to do, the harder it is to change.

- Teamwork gives you twice the results for half the effort.
- Do not let what you cannot do interfere with what you can.
- Humor is always the shortest distance between two people.
- Anyone can make a mistake, but to really mess things up requires a computer.
- People always have two reasons for doing things: a good reason and the real reason.
- People who think they know it all are a pain in the neck to those of us who really do.
- An expert is someone who knows more and more about less and less until he knows everything about nothing.

Intonation is a good indicator of how you feel about what you are saying. Look at the following contrasts. Notice how your voice tends to rise when you make a positive point and fall when you make a negative one.

- We are doing well in Europe, but not in the Middle East.
- Turnover is down, but productivity is up, and for the second year running.
- In Mexico we are number one, in Argentina we are number one, in Chile we are number one, but in Brazil we are nowhere.

Some things to do on your own:

- Keep a list of the 10 longest or most difficult words you use in your line of work or field of interest. Mark the stress for each word so you know exactly how to say it.

- Get used to editing your presentations to eliminate filler words, non-words, jargon, acronyms, sexist language, and hidden messages.
- Rehearse!

Mastering Your Material

Rehearsals allow you to feel comfortable with your presentation material. If you are rehearsing by yourself, play the devil's advocate and **ask yourself hard questions**. Imagine what you would say if you were in the audience.

Ask someone to role play what the decision maker might ask. If you find yourself stumbling at any point in the presentation, it may be that you do not truly believe your argument or that you missed some flaw in the logic when you organized the presentation. Go back to your presentation plan and check.

Your **choice of words** also reveals your mastery of the material. Rehearsals will give you the confidence to choose the strongest appropriate words. You will not be afraid to express yourself, for example, in clear, direct terms such as, "Continuing on this course will be destructive," rather than, "This course of action may present problems."

Your delivery will have much more meaning and power if you use **precise, strong language**. Once you have used a good, powerful word, though, do not get stuck on it. Calling three concepts "pivotal" in the same presentation dissipates the force of the word, and thus your argument. **Do not exaggerate**, either. Even one exaggerated statement makes a group suspicious, and a stream of overdone claims will undermine your whole argument.

Add Punch to Your Presentation

The Power of Threes

As you consider material that will develop your arguments, stay focused on your original objective. **Restrict your agenda to one specific situation or problem.** Avoid wandering off to discuss other items that may be on your personal agenda but are not relevant to your stated purpose.

Psychological studies tell us that people can remember between three and seven items at one time. Busy people or those under a lot of stress are likely to remember only **three items**.

If you give your audience too many reasons to buy your product or implement your idea, they may only remember a few of them, and not necessarily your most important or persuasive points. Therefore, if you have a lot of points to cover, **group them together** for easier recall. For example, a new marketing process may actually have 11 or 12 steps, but if you group them into categories such as design steps, packaging steps, and sales steps, they will be easier to follow.

Similarly, in a problem-solving pattern, there may be seven individual problems. If you group them into personnel problems and logistics problems, your presentation has been simplified, and the problems will be easier to remember. **Experienced speakers** know that there is power in threes of anything. Julius Caesar said, "I came, I saw, I conquered." Winston Churchill was a master at tripling. Many of his most powerful speeches to the people of Britain made use of this classic technique.

Think of all the examples there are in our lives and our literature: Three Blind Mice, Three Musketeers, and popular series of books that are written as trilogies. Leverage the knowledge about threes to give impact to your presentation.

Visual Aids

Think about using some visual aids in your presentations, and think beyond PowerPoint. PowerPoint has been a great tool, but also misused so frequently that bad presentations get called "**death by PowerPoint.**"

Visuals help you give a lot of information in a very short space of time. They are really quick snapshots of situations, developments, events, and processes that would take a long time to explain fully in words.

Good visuals speak for themselves and require little or no description, but you often need to draw your audience's attention to **one or two key points**.

The effect of good visuals can be ruined by reading them word for word. Instead, refer to the highlights (the most significant part), explain why they are important, and help the audience draw conclusions.

Here are some more **tips**:
- Be generous with white space.
- Use clear headings and sub-headings.
- Highlight, but do not overdo it.

- Types of highlighting can include bullets, italic print, underlining, bold, and color.
- Use graphics with caution. Make sure they mean the same thing to the audience that they do to you. Make sure that they look okay when on a screen, since they can get distorted when enlarged. Make sure you have legally purchased the rights to use any copyrighted material, including clip art and stock photography. Most can be used for personal reasons, but not commercially unless you purchase the rights to do so.
- Do not ask technology to do your job. Technology should support the presentation you deliver, but not be responsible for the success of the presentation.
- Always have a backup plan in case the technology fails, because oftentimes it will!

About type styles and size:

- Choose a solid, plain typeface that is easy to read.
- Do not combine a lot of fonts on one page. If you do use different fonts, use them consistently. Designers tell us that we should not have more than two different fonts per page.
- Make sure the type size is big enough for your audience to read.
- Do not use all capital letters, except in headings or brief statements.
- Headings should be noticeably larger than text.
- Serif typefaces, with hooks on each letter, make text easier to read.

Here is a chart detailing the various methods of adding some punch to your presentation. Remember, you should ALWAYS have a backup plan!

Type	Advantage	Disadvantage	Notes
Slides	Quality images Efficient Reusable Can embed video	Cost for stock photography/clip art Take time to prepare Projector not always available	Focus Make sure they are properly saturated (deep color)
Whiteboard	Inexpensive Flexible	Not impressive Smell of markers Dirties hands	Write neatly Have eraser handy and extra markers
DVD	Stimulating to audience May be supplied free of charge by public libraries	Audiences drift Tricky to run	May want to cue to several instances, rather than whole film

	Can insert DVD clips directly into slides		
Flip Charts	Pre-writing makes them easy to use Available everywhere	Too small for more than 20 people Wasting paper?	Use top 2/3 of page only 5×5 rule Practice writing
Handouts	Inexpensive Flexible Easy to prepare	Take time to prepare Wasting paper?	Must look professional Proofread
Models	Effective if notes attached	May get lost if passed around Difficult to find appropriate ones Expensive to buy	Must be visible

Benefit for target audience

_____

_____

_____

_____

Body
Point 1 (with statistics or examples)

_____

_____

_____

_____

Point 2 (with statistics or examples)

_____

_____

_____

_____

Point 3 (with statistics or examples)

_____

_____

_____

_____

Conclusion

Summary

Specific action

Strong final statement

CHAPTER 6

INFLUENCE AND PERSUASION

"It is not failure itself hat holds you back; it is the fear of failure that paralyzes you" – Brian Tracy

How Persuasion Works

Are you easily persuaded? If someone tries to talk you into something and is using all the powers of influence, what is your reaction?

When you are ready to buy something particular, you may find yourself more easily persuaded than at other times. However, when it comes to activities other than making purchases, we are often exposed to more subtlety. Choosing paint colors for your home or office where there is consensus required can result in more people trying to persuade you of one particular color or another. Or, perhaps you are the one who prefers to be convincing others, and are presenting clear arguments to get what you would like. People who successfully persuade to make a living include salespeople, fundraisers, recruiters, and advertisers. It is helpful to consider the techniques they use in order to be successful.

While there are plenty of techniques that people employ, research conducted by Robert Cialdini over many years became the focus of his excellent book *Influence: The Psychology of Persuasion*. The factors that he associates with persuasion are discussed below.

Predictability

People respond to what they expect. If they get a coupon, they expect that they are getting a reduced price, even when the terms of the coupon don't necessarily mean that is the case. If they know that one store is usually cheaper than the other, they tend to buy without checking prices closely. This principle also reflects the impression that high prices are associated with quality products, even though the product may not change.

Reciprocation

This principle describes how we respond by giving back one thing when we are given something else, especially a gift. This is something we see when people send thank-you notes after receiving a gift, as well as the offer of taking a new car for a test drive before you buy it. (Since the salesperson has been kind enough to arrange a ride – a gift – the purchaser may be more receptive to the car.)

Some other examples:
- If your neighbors invite you over for a meal, you return the gesture.
- If a friend invites your child to a birthday party, you return the gesture for their child when it is your child's birthday.

After we make a decision, our actions will support the choice we made even when we are faced with the knowledge that a better choice might have been a good idea, or when we have to wait a long time for delivery. When it comes to creating gaming systems and smartphones, manufacturers know that they can market the next release as soon as the last one is on the store shelves because their customers do not just need one gaming system or one smartphone. They want to keep up with what is new and they want to use current, leading edge products that meet their needs.

Social Evidence

Marketers work with what works. Although many people dislike the idea of a laugh track (a pre-recorded loop of people laughing that gets played in many television comedies), marketers know that the laugh track engages people in the program. Laugh tracks even help engage listeners when the jokes are bad! The canned laughter makes us laugh because it triggers a response that says, "Hey, you are supposed to find this funny!" And so, we laugh.

We respond to statements that something is a "best-selling" item, even though the tag line does not tell us anything about the quality of the item. If you have ever watched a telethon for public television or a charity, you've seen the screen roll with names of everyone who donated, which is a way of saying to people, "Hey, look at what your neighbors are doing. Your name needs to be here too!"

Authority

We tend to believe people who are in positions of authority and trust, whether they actually earned that trust or not. We trust doctors, police, and firefighters. We also trust actors who are dressed as people with authority. Actors do shampoo, makeup, and beauty promotions, and people buy the products even when the claims are unproven or the products are toxic, because we want to believe that they know what they are talking about.

Liking

You already know that you will buy from or be convinced of something by people that you like. This is the likeability factor. Customers will return to shop at stores with friendly or attentive staff because they are likeable, even if the prices are a little higher than the competition if the competition provides lousy service.

Home shopping parties such as Tupperware, Pampered Chef, Epicure, and others have capitalized enormously on the likeability factor. Instead of buying from an unknown sales person, people come to the party to put up with a demonstration, flip through catalogs, look at samples, win prizes, and buy products. While the salesperson is really the one selling, party goers spend in order to support the hostess, who also happens to be their friend. The friends know that the more money that they spend, the more "free" benefits that the hostess receives in exchange for hosting the party. People at the party are well aware of this, and will also leverage reciprocity by asking this particular hostess to attend the party that they book.

Scarcity

Scarcity is a great technique to drive people's need to have things. Commercials promote upcoming products, and manufacturers will deliberately release small quantities in order to drive up interest in the product. They will even use excuses like having design challenges, materials challenges, or something equally ambiguous. Meanwhile, customers are trying to find one of the scarce copies in order to be part of the special group that has the product.

If you collect loyalty points, you see scarcity at work when the program offers its members a "deal," like being able to buy a highly desirable smartphone that you can only get with the program and is not available in any store. People without enough points can combine points and cash to purchase the item, but unless you are a member of the program, you will not be able to participate.

Self-Interest

Everything that we undertake includes some component of self-interest, and persuaders are very conscious of this. As a standard, people want to get (or believe they have) a good value, and even a great deal, every time they invest energy or spend money on something. Even people who volunteer for altruistic reasons often understand the virtue of reciprocity for their good deeds.

Preparing to Persuade

Pushing and Pulling

Pushing and pulling are two ways of applying influence, and both of them have a place in persuasion. People prefer to make choices and decide what they want, so they are mostly inclined to where they are pulled. However, when used together, pushing will help to influence people to make a break away from what's familiar in order to try something that they are pulled to.

Sometimes people are stuck in a position, and helping them to break away (whether it involves them changing their mind, setting new goals, or learning new skills) can then make them more ready and open to being pulled in a particular direction.

Pushing is about *selling,* whereas pulling is about *telling.* In business practices we could create an analogy by saying that pushing is used by managers, whereas pulling is used by leaders.

Pulling is more difficult than pushing, but it is more effective in terms of lasting results. When we push, we have no idea where the person will go, other than away from something. On the other hand, pulling has one direction: toward something. Pulling is accomplished by creating desire in the other person, working with what you know about what the other person wants, and understanding the way in which they will decide what they want.

To push, you need some kind of influence over the other person so that they make a shift. This is normally accomplished because you have that person's trust or you have authority over things that they need. The level of authority you have needs to be high enough (or strong enough) that they are obligated to do what you are asking or telling them. At work, this can include the power to fire, demote, or transfer someone to another role. A supervisor is pushing when they tell employees what to do, as opposed to providing an opportunity for them to make choices and their own decisions.

Physical pushing also has a role in the business environment. Security, police forces, and the military can use physical power to get what they need accomplished. This can include the physical removal of unruly employees, as well as protestors on your property, although it can have a lot of negative publicity attached to it.

Learn how to use push and pull in your persuasion so that you can help to create desire or emotional attachment, while helping others to break away from unhelpful behaviors or old patterns.

Persuasion relies on communication skills. As well, we can gain more of what we want and send stronger messages when we do so confidently. A manager or leader who appears wishy-washy has no influence over their staff. A child having a temper tantrum, on the other hand, has confidence that they are absolutely correct.

Confidence also requires that you have credibility with your audience or employee. People will not listen nor be persuaded by someone they are unable to trust. To be trusted, we have to act in a trustworthy manner. This means that we do what we say we will do, when we say we will do it. It also means that we know and operate under a system of ethics and that people know what those ethics are.

While not all conversations can be planned ahead, there are many conversations that benefit from a **plan**. When you prepare yourself before initiating a conversation, you are much more likely to deliver an effective message that doesn't get misunderstood, and to deliver it to the right person. Here are some steps that you can take to prepare yourself.

Have a purpose.

Typical purposes for a conversation are to inform or direct, to persuade, or to ask a question.

Have an outcome.

Ask yourself a few questions to help you decide how to approach the conversation:

- What reaction are you looking for from the listener?
- What do you need the listener to remember?
- What do you need the listener to do after your conversation?

Make sure the receiver is ready.

Some people resent it when we pounce on them unannounced. Others are much more receptive when you simply ask permission. If you are unsure if someone is ready to talk, try these helpful icebreakers:

- Is this a good time to talk?
- Can we talk about something I've been thinking about?
- Would now be a good time to talk, or should I come back later?
- Can I have 15 minutes of your time? (Make sure you stick to just 15 minutes!)

Apply positive intent.

Positive intent means that you have good reasons for saying and doing what you do, and so do other people. If we assume that other people have negative intentions behind their actions, we can create a negative environment where that is the eventual outcome. This can make it very hard to work cooperatively. You will have to practice positive intent yourself and use your communication for good intentions, while assuming that others have that same positive intention. This ultimately means that we avoid making negative assumptions and statements, that we avoid gossip, and that we focus on the future rather than the past.

Self-concept, self-image, and self-esteem can all impact the way that we send and receive messages. Individuals with low self-esteem and a negative self-image tend to operate in a passive style. Other people might think that they are superior to everyone else, resulting in an aggressive style. This creates all kinds of interesting conversations!

Words to Watch Out For

If you want to be known for clear communication, avoid words like:

- I'll try
- Ought to
- Should have
- Must
- Always
- Never

If you are tempted to insert these words into your conversations, replace them with clearer terms. Instead of "I'll try to get back to you later," say "I'll call you back by 4:00 today" (and then make sure that you do!).

Your Inner Self Talk

Be aware of the internal messages you give yourself. If you start from a negative self-concept and negative expectations, your external behavior will likely be non-assertive and you may end up feeling frustrated or angry. The more you replace your self-talk with positive, confident words, the more confident you become. We know that is easily said, and more difficult to realize, but it's worth the results! This helps you build credibility and trust with the people you speak with, since your words and actions will be congruent.

Frame of Reference

A **frame of reference** is a way in which we judge other people. We all make judgments about people, but in order to really get the meaning of what's going on, we need to be able to suspend those judgments and let their meaning come to us unfettered. A communicator's ability to suspend their frame of reference is a critical and important skill because it can build their credibility and make them a more effective communicator.

Your frame of reference is made up of your beliefs, assumptions, values, feelings, judgments, emotions, advice, moods, thoughts, biases, and stress levels at any given moment. Because your frame of reference is so personal and so deeply embedded, it is very difficult to practice suspending it on a regular basis. We all interpret reality from our own vantage point and sometimes we react in a self-serving manner. We have to learn to take others' points of view and feelings, as well as our own, into consideration.

How can we do this? Try to:

- Put others before yourself

- Check things out before jumping to conclusions, making assumptions, or reacting emotionally
- Give others the benefit of the doubt

Suspension of belief is especially appropriate when others need to be understood in order for their tension or stress to be defused.

Think about suspending belief in these situations:
- A police officer who arrives on a violent scene where everyone has a weapon, but someone is declaring their innocence.
- A scene at work where workers are bullying a co-worker. The person who appears to be the victim, however, is a known bully.
- You put your lunch in the fridge when you arrived at work this morning, but when you look in your lunch bag, half the lunch is missing.
- You reach for the last loaf of bread in the bakery at the same time as someone else. The other person looks harried, but otherwise very similar to you.

Matching and Mirroring

There are a few different ways to create and strengthen rapport. Once you have established a basic connection and a mutual sense of trust, then you can work on developing and deepening rapport.

You must use these methods in a discreet manner to avoid irritating or insulting the other person. Not every technique is appropriate in every situation. As well, keep in mind that these are just guidelines, not hard and fast rules.

One of the easiest ways to develop rapport is to mirror or match the other person's body language and non-verbal signals. We can't stress how important it is to do this subtly so that the other person doesn't feel like they're talking to a parrot! Let's look at some of the techniques that you can try.

Body Language

It is generally very easy to subtly **match** another person's body language, such as their posture, breathing rate, and gestures. If they lean back, you might do the same (subtly, a few moments after they do so). Or, you might perform a **reciprocal movement**; that is, if you start tapping your pencil, I might subtly start tapping my foot in the same rhythm. You might even **mirror** them; if they tilt their head to the left, you might tilt your head to the right.

Of course, you should only mirror the aspects of their body language that feel natural to you.

You also need to keep your own body language in line with what you are saying. If you are saying that you are interested, but your body is leaning away, your eyes are roaming around the room, or you are tapping your foot, you do not look interested at all and your body language in inconsistent with your message.

Voice Characteristics

Never, ever attempt to do an imitation of a person's voice or to match their accent. This is almost always insulting. You can, however, mimic some basic voice features, including:

- Volume of their voice
- Speed (fast or slow)
- Tone (high or low)

Pacing

Pacing techniques can help you achieve a deeper level of rapport. Part of pacing is the matching and mirroring techniques that we just discussed. Another part is including true statements in your conversation to give more credibility to other statements. (Research shows that you must use at least three true statements in a row for this to work.) Hearing several true statements in a row also lowers their guard and makes them more open to agreeing with you.

Imagine that you're at a seminar listening to a sales pitch.

Scenario One

The speaker starts out with, "Thanks for coming! I'm going to tell you about my new product that you'll love."

Does that grab your attention? Are you convinced that you'll love this product?

Scenario Two

Now let's try this. The speaker says:

- It's a beautiful sunny morning!

- It's really early.
- We've all come here for a reason.

Then, he might move into some more speculative statements:

- I know you're all happy to be here.
- I imagine that you're interested in my new product.
- I bet that you would like to do more in less time.

Now he might introduce the statements that are new to you:

- You are going to love this product.
- You won't want to wait to get your hands on this.

How do you feel now?

Leading

Once you have established rapport, you might be able to influence the other person's behavior without them realizing it! Test this with a small gesture, like adjusting your posture or tugging your earlobe. If the person mirrors or matches your gesture in some way, you're all set to continue leading! If not, you'll need to deepen rapport some more.

If the person that you are communicating with is now in a receptive state, you can use your body language to influence their state of mind. For example, if they seem to be in a dissociative state, you can try leaning forward and using more gestures (both associative behaviors) to move them to an associative state.

Remember that the key is to incorporate influencing behaviors subtly and naturally so that the other person isn't offended or annoyed.

Using Stories to Persuade

The Importance of Story

As human beings, we are wired for stories. We don't often hold a whole list of items or facts for long, but we will remember the gist of a good story for a lifetime. Metaphors and analogies are often a part of storytelling.

Using stories can help make your point more memorable and easier to understand. This makes them a helpful persuasive tool. In his book *All Marketers Are Liars*, Seth Godin talks about the power of a story to draw in customers and to persuade. He also shares some things we can learn.

Stories have to make you stand out.

If you simply repeat someone else's story and try to make it sound original, it won't. If you are trying to convince your spouse that a holiday to the Mediterranean is in order, and it is the same story your friends are telling each other, you won't be very convincing. Tell your story.

7-Up called their product "the un-Cola" to differentiate from all of the cola drinks in the marketplace. You have to find something that helps you stand out from the crowd. If there is nothing that makes your story stand out from all the others, your results won't stand out either.

Your story has to be believable.

If your story is not true, your results won't appear. You cannot persuade by telling lies, can you? Well, actually you can! This is why people buy garbage from watching infomercials; they become convinced that this particular gadget will do what they need, make them look like they want, or bring them some kind of status. The reason that stories that actually lie still persuade people is because sometimes people want to agree with you. Once they do agree to something, they do not like to be proven wrong.

Storytelling works when it makes something more.

If you believe storytelling, then you may believe that a different glass makes your wine taste better. Does food cooked in cookware endorsed by a famous chef taste better than that cooked in the same product without an endorsement? If you believe the story that comes with it, it sure does!

Have a beginning, middle, and end.

A story is not the same thing as a paragraph or an argument. A story is complete, with a beginning, middle, and an end. Using this format will help your story to be memorable and to carry your meaning.

Be conscious of our attention span.

While we are wired to respond to and appreciate stories, we've also become accustomed to short messages on billboards and text messages. Remember your audience and think about capturing their attention without giving them license to be distracted as you deliver your message.

Insightful Sentences

Another way of moving others towards a desired outcome is by using language that presupposes that you know what they are thinking.

Some **insightful sentence stems** that you can use:

- You might be thinking…
- You're probably wondering…
- You're probably asking yourself…
- I can predict your next move.
- I know what you are thinking/will say.
- You will likely have an answer.

Once again, it is important to use these techniques appropriately. A sales pitch that includes the statement, "You might be wondering how this product can save you time," isn't terribly presumptuous. But starting a pitch with, "I can predict your next move: you will buy this product!" might irritate some of your potential clients!

Overcoming Challenges

Another way of getting the outcome you want is by learning how to **break down oppositional thinking**. For example, let's say that you are trying to convince your accountant to hire some help for the upcoming tax season. He says, "Those people never do anything right."

You could ask him to **clarify** several parts of that statement:

- Who are "those people?" ("Everyone" is not an answer!)
- Is "never" really true? If the person in question has never prepared a proper tax return, perhaps they should not be an accountant!

- What is the definition of "right?" Is the accountant talking about legally correct or simply the way he would do it?

The goal here is to help the person explore their negative thinking and look at the bigger picture, instead of seeing things through a particular lens.

Ten Ways to Persuade

1. Demonstrate your expertise and knowledge without becoming patronizing.
2. Make sure integrity is reflected in your standards, values, and behavior.
3. Know when to be silent.
4. Create an obligation for one or both parties.
5. Proceed a bit at a time, from inconsequential points into major areas.
6. Never corner people. Leave them a way out.
7. Give sincere compliments.
8. Be childlike: open and transparent. Expand your center of interests to include others and explore the talents of others.
9. Remember names.
10. Remember: difficult people don't play by the same rules.

(Adapted from the *Secrets of Power Persuasion* by Roger Dawson)

Negotiation Techniques

The essence of negotiating is that in order to get what we want, sometimes we have to give something up. We can negotiate on price (you give me more value and I will give you more money) or principles.

Argue Based on Principle instead of Positions

You've probably heard that expression that someone is "digging their heels in," meaning that they are so focused on what they want (and their position) that they have lost sight of the topic being argued and the principle.

If you are negotiating, try not to defend a position; otherwise you simply become more attached to it and will defend it even harder. You'll try to save face and lose your commitment to the real problem.

Arguing Chips Away at Relationships

Since a negotiation is a form of conversation, the idea is to have successful negotiations that contribute to more conversations. Be careful that your approach to negotiating does lead to a battle of wills. Each of you can clearly state what you are willing to do or not do, and then work through the problem rather than deteriorating to personal attacks and bravado.

The Softer Side

Sometimes people who resist conflict or who understand the high price that can be exacted for hard bargaining try to soften the edge by being friendlier in their approach. They get focused on the relationship and on reaching an agreement rather than simply pushing their own agenda. This is an example of soft negotiation where we extend trust to the other side, make offers and concessions, and do what we can to avoid confrontation.

Principled Negotiation Works

Instead of having to choose whether to stick to your position, or to use a soft or hard positional approach, we recommend that you apply **principled negotiation**. This approach is neither soft nor hard, and works in almost any negotiation by applying four simple strategies, as described in *Getting to Yes* by Roger Fisher and William Ury.

Each point deals with a basic element of negotiation and suggests what you should do about it.

- **People**: Focus on the problem, not the people.
- **Interests**: Be concerned with interests of both parties, not digging in your heels.
- **Options**: Think of different solutions and possibilities instead of starting out from where you want to end up.
- **Standard**: Make sure that results are based on an actual standard, instead of something subjective.

Focus on the Problem, Not the People

We often make the comment that we have to focus on behaviors, not people. Take this concept seriously. Don't get angry: get clear about behaviors that need to change.

Negotiators are People First

When it comes to negotiations, we are dealing with human beings. And when people get passionate about something, it is a good reminder for us to see that they have emotions, convictions, different paradigms, and they can be unpredictable.

When things get heated, which they will at times, remember that your emotions and hot buttons are also involved. Ask yourself if you are paying attention to the people, or are getting distracted by positions.

Expressing Your No

Once you understand what someone is asking of you and decide you want to say no, choose the kind of no that best suits the person and situation. Here are some general rules to follow.

Say no **firmly and calmly**, without saying, "I'm sorry," which weakens your position.

Say no, followed by a **straightforward explanation** of what you are feeling or what you are willing to do.
- "I'm uncomfortable doing that."
- "I'm not willing to do that."
- "I don't want to do that."
- "I don't like to do that."

Say no, and then give a **choice or alternative**.
- "I can't help you now, but I will when I get this done, which could be in an hour."
- "I don't have time today, but I could help out the first thing tomorrow morning."

Say no and then **clarify your reasons**. This does not include long-winded statements filled with excuses, justifications, and rationalizations. It's enough that you do not want to say yes. Your clarification is given to provide the receiver more information so that he or she can better understand your position.

Use your **natural no**. You may have developed your own style of saying no based on your past experience and personality. If so, use it.

Make an **empathetic listening statement** and then say no. You may paraphrase the content and feeling of the request, and then state your no.

Example: "I can see that it is important to you that one of my assistants gets your report done. I'd like to have someone do it, but my staff is already overburdened with high priority tasks to be completed by the end of the day."

Say yes, and then give your **reasons for not doing it or your alternative solution**. This approach is very interesting. You may want to use it in situations when you are willing to meet the request, but not at the time or in the way the other person wants it.
"Yes, I would be willing to help you out, but I won't have time until this afternoon."
"Yes, I'd be willing to go along with your second alternative, but not the third one you suggested."

The Persistent Response

You can also use the persistent response. This method of saying no entails using a one-sentence refusal statement and persistently repeating it as often as necessary, no matter what the person says. This technique is useful when dealing with very aggressive or manipulative people who won't take no for an answer. The persistent response can be effective in maintaining your refusal while continuing to be in charge of your emotions.

Because this way of saying no is unusual and a bit complex, we will provide some detailed guidelines for applying it.

First, select a concise, one-sentence statement and repeat it no matter what the other person says or does. Examples:
"I understand how you feel, but I'm not willing…"
"I'm not interested…"
"I don't want to…'"
"I'm uncomfortable doing that, so I don't want to…"
"You might be right, but I'm not interested."

After each statement by the other person, say your persistent response sentence. It's important that you don't get sidetracked by responding to any other issue the other person brings up.

Guidelines for Saying No

Say your statement **firmly, calmly, and as unemotionally** as possible.

Be aware of your **nonverbal behavior**, making sure you don't come across passively or aggressively. Use plenty of **silence** to your advantage. Your silence will project the message that the other's statements and manipulation are futile.

Be **persistent**. Simply state your response one more time than the other person makes his or her request, question, or statement. If the other person makes six statements, you make seven. If the other person makes three statements, you make four. Most often, the other person will feel ill at ease and stop after three or four statements. Other times, your response will move the other person to offer options you are willing to go along with.

Getting to the Heart of the Problem

If you think of the assessment you completed in Session Three, you classified yourself on a scale of assertiveness and emotionality.

Dealing with challenging people (or difficult people, depending on how you define things), can be scary if you are a conflict avoider, but we are going to run into challenging people throughout our lives, so it's best to have a great set of tools to manage these issues.

For example, you might be a supervisor who had to speak with an employee about some unacceptable behavior. Perhaps they are always late for work, even though they are supposed to be answering the phones at 8:00 a.m.

You've spoken with the employee a couple of times, and this led to improved punctuality for a few days before he slipped back to being late again. You have even spoken to your human resources consultant about suspending the employee, but they think that suspension is too harsh a punishment, despite your thorough record-keeping that shows how often and how bad this behavior is.

You've been braver than plenty of workplace leaders because you have discussed the problem with the employee and with HR. But somehow, the behavior continues, and you get a sense that you are not doing enough.

What's Missing?

You aren't getting to the heart of the problem. It's not enough to tell the individual that they are breaking the rules, or that a colleague has to cover their tasks when they are late. If it were enough, the behavior would stop.

Ask yourself what is really bothering *you* to get at what is really bothering *them*. Often the behavior touches a nerve that is much more personal. For example, if you hired the receptionist because he was the son of a friend, and you felt that he was taking advantage of your relationship with him and his parents by not caring about the schedule, that's at a much deeper level than just the rules that are being broken.

If the person is perpetually late because they do not set their alarm (and get up to it) because they really do not care about their job, or they feel underutilized, or they are being bullied by a co-worker and cannot drag themselves into the office, then we are getting at the root of the real problem.
If you are content to only deal with the surface issues, and you are afraid to dig and get at the deeper issues, you will not be a part of improving the situation. You simply scrape the moss off of the surface, only to have it to grow back later.

The ability to peel an infraction back to its core takes patience and precision. Sometimes we don't do this because it can take time to uncover the real problem. We can often find ourselves in too much of a hurry to do this properly. At other times, our emotions get involved and we make a decision that we really don't want to go there because we'll also have to deal with what is bothering us.

If you don't stop to think about the big picture, you'll end up either missing the problem or going after too many problems at one. To stop yourself from being over-involved, you must be able to state the problem in a single sentence. If you make it longer, you'll lose focus of the real problem.

The Three F's

To get to the heart of the problem, evaluate the 3 F's: **facts**, **frequency**, and **frustrated relationship**.

Facts

What are the facts of the issue? Create a list so that you do not get sidetracked while you plan your conversation. Don't drag in other stories or unrelated issues that have happened previously. If you are talking to someone about tardiness, then stick to that and leave things like poor report writing, gossiping, or not taking care of equipment out of the conversation.

Frequency

Make sure you have a very clear history of the frequency of the issue. In this case, how often is the individual late? How late are they?

Describe the pattern like this: "This is the second time that I've called this to your attention. You agreed it would not happen again. Now I am concerned that I cannot trust you to keep a promise."

Revealing that you notice a pattern brings the history to the forefront. The history is important because repeated frequency erodes your trust.

Frustrated Relationship

If your real concern is about the relationship, but you only focus on the pattern, then you are not likely to get the change that you are aiming for. You have to discuss what is

187

important to you in terms of the relationship. Explain that when they repeatedly ignore your expectations to be on time, they aren't just demonstrating a lack of commitment to the job. They are eroding your trust in them, your trust in their ability to do their job, and the possibility of being trusted with assignments in the future.

Comments like the following can be helpful:

- I feel like I cannot trust you to get the work done.
- I feel like I am constantly nagging you and I don't like to do that.
- I feel like I can't trust you to keep the commitments you make.

CHAPTER 7

YOUR PERSONAL BRAND

Abigail Van Buren, the writer of Dear Abby, once said,

"There are two kinds of people: those who come into a room with the attitude, 'Here I am!' and those who have the attitude, 'There you are!'"

This chapter explores the type of impact we want to have in life and work. You will consider and define the influence you can have on these areas and learn skills for success and how to create those circumstances.

The Importance of a Personal Brand

What's in a Brand?
Companies brand themselves to create an image, a recognizable spark that encourages their target customers to connect with them, remember them, and do business with them. We create a personal image for the same reason; to build a brand centered on ourselves that leads people to think of us.

Have you thought about the impact you can be having when you do things? What do you want people to think of when you network with them, sell to them, consult or help them, or when you come to them looking for business, a job, or whatever it is that you need? What is it you do that makes you, or your work, stand out in other people's minds?

Whatever the stand-out factor is, it becomes part of your personal brand.

While we all define success in a way that means something to us personally, we often look to others for inspiration and ideas. Whether success to you means earning recognition; making money; or achieving education, financial, career, emotional, or other goals, this course will give you tools you need to take yourself there as a reflection of your personal brand.

Brand Elements

Elements of your personal brand include your entire package, such as:

- Body language
- Image (including how you dress, your hair, and accessories)
- Communication skills
- Credibility
- Managing difficult situations
- Social media presence

In commercial terms, a brand is the customer's perception of a product. Organizations build that perception by paying attention to areas such as:

- Product development
- Research and innovation
- Marketing
- Sales
- Return on investment
- Bottom line

- Finances in the black or red
- Community involvement

In reality, though, the brand is the consumer's perception and nothing more. In a similar way, your **personal brand** is people's perception about you. People who do business with you have pretty high expectations about what a particular brand provides them, and they will review all aspects of you to form their perception.

Having a personal brand doesn't mean that you have to dress in the same uniform every day (although you might dress in a consistent pattern), or that you are an eccentric individual (although you may be). It doesn't mean that if you are an introvert you must become gregarious, and it does not require that the extroverts mask their feelings or thoughts about things.

Brand Style Assessment

Choose the phrase that most closely reflects the way you see yourself (not the way you want others to see you). Sometimes you may feel that more than one statement fits; if that happens, choose the one that is most like you most of the time.

1. **When I meet someone at a cocktail reception, I like to:**
   a. Learn lots about them
   b. Tell them about myself
   c. See what's on the food table
   d. Hover on the fringe, observing, and interacting as people approach

191

2. When I attend a networking event or workshop, I usually:

a. Listen attentively to all introductions

b. Don't need to be introduced; we all have name tags

c. I listen to most of them, but if they are too long-winded my attention drifts elsewhere

d. I avoid these events because I have too much else to do

3. When I am in a managerial or leadership role:

a. People on my team come to me for direction

b. I check every step of the project

c. I encourage them to be independent

d. I avoid giving negative performance reviews

4. When I go to a meeting, I usually:

a. Volunteer to take notes

b. Sit near the meeting chair, but avoid taking notes

c. Sit with a least one seat between me and the next person

d. Sit beside another person

5. When I meet someone I know fairly well:

a. I ask about how their day is going

b. I share a story or a joke

c. I get right to the point

d. I introduce the conversation by outlining its purpose

6. When I am at a meeting and someone is doing a presentation:

a. I want it to bring a few laughs

b. I try to imagine how the presenter feels
c. I try to analyze the logic of what's being discussed
d. I get bored or impatient if it does not flow well or engage me

7. **When people enter my work space or home, I usually:**
a. Invite them to sit down
b. Tell them to sit down
c. Let them decide where or whether they want to sit
d. Pull out a chair for them

8. **When I am speaking with people:**
a. I prefer to stand close to them
b. I like to keep three feet or more of distance between us
c. I need to have room to step back if they get too close
d. I don't mind if they are close to me

9. **When I deliver a presentation, it:**
a. Is well organized
b. Connects to people on an emotional level
c. Is powerful
d. Is entertaining

10. **My telephone calls:**
a. Are almost non-existent now; I text for efficiency
b. Avoid small talk and focus on purpose
c. Are animated and lively
d. Tend to be quite long

11. **Publicly speaking on a cell phone:**

a. Keeps life interesting
b. Makes most people uncomfortable
c. Helps me learn what people are thinking about
d. Should be avoided

12. When my work group celebrates a big win, I tend to:

a. Attend the party
b. Organize the party and invite everyone
c. Focus on the time and money it involves
d. Avoid the party if possible, but put in an appearance if I have to

13. Which of the following interests you the most?

a. Ideas
b. Information
c. People
d. Actions

14. You respect when you and others pay attention to:

a. Intelligence
b. Authority
c. Relationships
d. Performance

15. You pride yourself on being able to:

a. Solve problems
b. Look after details
c. Inspire others to action
d. Make quick and effective decisions

Results Tabulation

Assessment Tool Results

Check your answer to each question in the Branding Style, and circle the answer below that relates to it. For example, if you selected statement A in question 1, you would circle the symbol beside 1a below. Once you have finished transferring your answers to this page, count the number of each symbol.

Scoring Guide				
1 a.○ b.□ c.→ d.△	2 a.○ b.△ c.□ d.→	3 a.△ b.→ c.□ d. ○	4 a.○ b.□ c.→ d.△	5 a.○ b.□ c.△ d.→
6 a.□ b.○ c.→ d.△	7 a.○ b.△ c.→ d.□	8 a.□ b.→ c.△ d.○	9 a.→ b.○ c.△ d.○	10 a.→ b.△ c.□ d.○
11 a.□ b.→ c.○ d.△	12 a.○ b.□ c.→ d.△	13 a.○ b.→ c.△ d.□	14 a.→ b.△ c.○ d.□	15 a.○ b.→ c.△ d.□

Totals

Δ   □   ○   →

_____   _____   _____   _____

_____   _____   _____   _____

Scoring

If you scored highest in the:

Δ category, your primary style is **Pragmatic**

□ category, your primary style is **Enthusiastic**

○ category, your primary style is **Accommodating**

→ category, your primary style is **Detailed**

Debrief

These results will give you a good idea of your self-perception: the way that you look and act in front of other people, which is the foundation for your personal brand. Keep in mind that while things can be in sharp contrast on paper, as people we are much more of a blend of all these types. Depending on how close our scores are, we can flex our behavior between styles (within our comfort and ability levels) to suit our purposes.

No one type is any better or worse than the other – they just provide us with a platform to talk about who we are and how we behave. If you scored within three points of another category, you may find it quite easy to stretch yourself and behave in the manner of that other category. If you are farther away, you will find stretching to appeal to people with other tendencies a little more challenging, but you can learn to get along with all kinds of people.

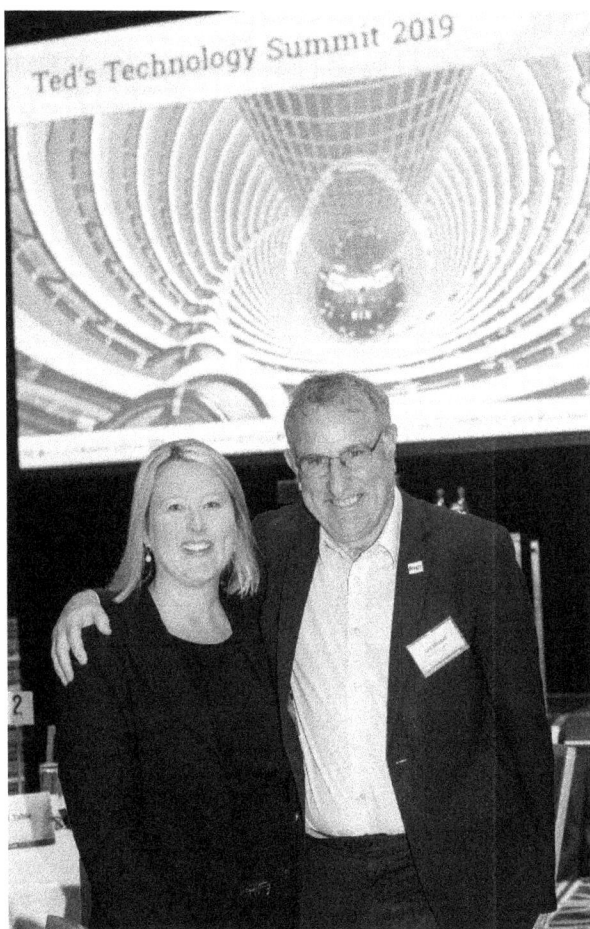

Brand Assessment Matrix

Here is a visual representation of the results of your assessment:

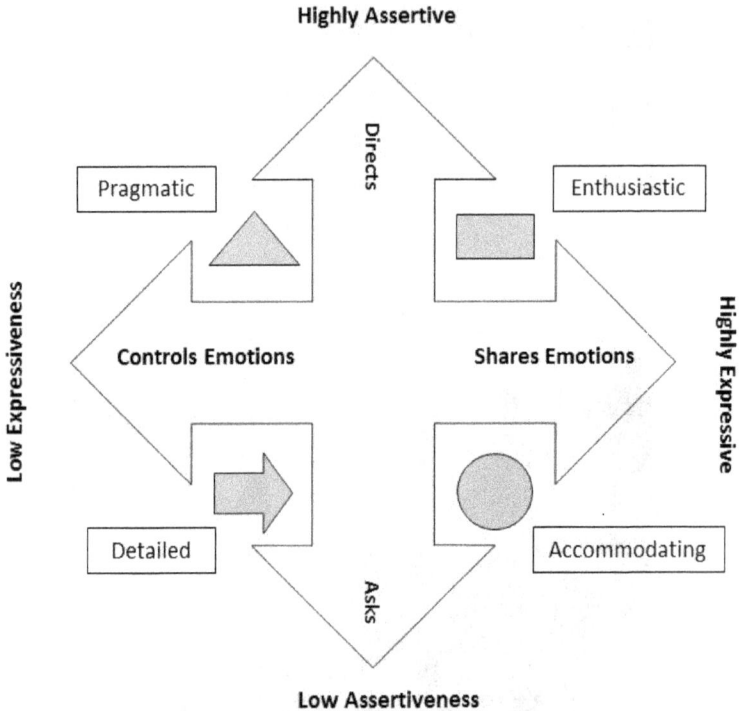

Highly Assertive

Directs

| Pragmatic | | Enthusiastic |

Controls Emotions **Shares Emotions**

Low Expressiveness

Highly Expressive

| Detailed | | Accommodating |

Asks

Low Assertiveness

Understanding Styles

Sometimes our approach needs to be adjusted in order to present our brand in a way that other people will resonate with. If, for example, you are pragmatic, you may find that people who are an accommodating style have the most trouble relating to you. You are more assertive than they are, and less expressive. They value expression in order to relate to people and have a need to have people understand one another. They are also less assertive than you, and if you have a tendency toward aggression, they will often avoid getting to know you.

The Pragmatic Style (Δ)

The pragmatic style is demonstrated by being highly assertive and lower in expressiveness (the top left quadrant in the diagram). The pragmatic style is characterized by decisiveness; direct, quick speech; loud tones; direct eye contact; a bold visual appearance; and a respect for personal distance. Your personal spaces at work, home, or the gym all denote a powerful presence. Your handshake is firm.

Strengths include getting to the heart of the matter quickly, being direct, and presenting a position strongly. Challenges include listening, demonstrating patience, a tendency to argue, and not taking the advice of others who have more experience or expertise to offer.

The Enthusiastic Style (□)

Enthusiasts express their emotions and are assertive; see the top right quadrant in the diagram. The enthusiastic style expresses opinions easily and can be very persuasive in their approach. They use a lot of inflection, expressive tones, and are animated when they speak. They tend to be active and demonstrate a lot of movement and enthusiasm about everything they do.

Their workspaces are often cluttered and they are comfortable with close physical proximity. Challenges can include listening and paying attention to details, a tendency to generalize frequently, and to exaggerate or be overly dramatic.

The Accommodating Style (○)

The accommodating style is characterized by a tendency to low assertiveness and high expressiveness. This style focuses on relationship integrity. They listen, use supportive language, and thrive when everyone is working well and without conflict. Their speech is often at a slow to moderate rate, using soft tones. They demonstrate patience, build trust, and use supportive language. They do not need to shake hands, although they will if that's what everyone else is doing. This style prefers to hug.

Their workspace will contain family pictures and sentimental items. Their challenges can include handling conflict when it does arise, keeping opinions to themselves, and dealing with data and figures.

The Detailed Style (→)

The detailed style is found in the lower left corner of the diagram and is depicted by low levels of assertiveness and low levels of expressiveness. This style focuses on details, facts, and figures. They use precise language and avoid bringing emotion into the conversation. They use little vocal inflection, speak economically, and control their emotions.

They will avoid touching (shaking hands and particularly hugging) if possible, and maintain a very strong sense of personal space. If there are things hanging in their office, they will be related to charts and graphs. Their desktop will be tidy and well-organized. Challenges can include being too focused on details and losing sight of the bigger picture, and not paying attention to people's feelings.

Business Etiquette

Having good manners doesn't just mean you make a positive impression; they are also good for business. No matter how formal or informal your personal brand is, people still care about social skills and manners (even if they don't come out and say so). Rules about which fork to use for the salad, or not talking with food in your mouth, are examples of **good manners**. **Etiquette**, however, takes the discussion about manners to a higher level.

Emily Post, famous for her approach to etiquette, manners, and ethics, defined etiquette like this: "Whenever two people come together and their behavior affects one another, you have etiquette. Etiquette is not some rigid code of manners; it's simply how persons' lives touch one another."

When you apply your awareness of etiquette in different situations, you demonstrate that you want to be taken seriously. You become an ambassador for what you do and who you work with.

How You Sound

Do you have a "**phone voice**?" This is the voice you always use when you answer the phone; there can be total chaos around you, but when you pick up the phone and say, "Good morning," the caller hears calm professionalism.

In contrast is the voice we use on the street or at the market. Some of us have grown up using what we might call "**street language**," or language that is commonly spoken with friends outside of the workplace. In business, however, we want to be clearly understood and so we apply a veneer or polish to our language. Sometimes a vocal or image coach will teach you to drop your street language so that it stops creeping into your business conversations and so that we are more easily understood.

When it comes to how you sound, you have to make a decision based on what's important to you and the brand you represent. Does your accent create a barrier in some way? If not, there is no need to change it. But if your accent prevents people from understanding you, or if your street language is having a negative impact on your brand, then it may be worth doing something about.

Things to Consider

Here are some things to consider when evaluating your business voice:

- What's your speech like?
- Do you have a position of authority and a very soft speaking voice? Is it helping you?
- Or, do you work with a lot of soft-spoken people and speak to them in a booming, direct voice?
- Do people listen to you?
- Do they respect you?
- How is your voice supporting the brand that you wish to project?

Developing Focus and Concentration

Getting Focused

Sometimes we have so much going on, it's as though we disrupt our own ability to concentrate and get things done. Whether you want to be known as a go-to person who does it all, or you are someone who gets things done through others, you must be able to complete projects in order to be credible and build your brand.

Sadly, some of us seem to look for the easiest way to getting things done. We put in just enough effort to avoid getting fired, or at least manage to avoid the performance talk with our boss. Taking the easy way out time and time again is an example of poor behavior. If you want to be recognized as someone who gets things done, and who has a positive impact on their workplace or their own company, you're going to have to work hard.

One way to accomplish a lot more than everyone else seems able to is to apply yourself with focus and concentration. This means that you clear distractions (from your desk or your mind), and you get to work.

The 80/20 Rule

The 80/20 Rule, or Pareto's law, says that 20% of what is on your to do list will bring 80% of your results. Make sure you are working on the 20% to make the most of your time. When it comes to the low value, time-consuming tasks, make sure that you delegate them, or take them off your list completely!

Improving Your Concentration and Confidence

Concentration is a skill that is learned and can be vastly improved. Many of us work in an environment of distractions and interruptions like e-mail notifications, the Internet, stimulants like coffee or soda, and meetings. All of these things interfere with our ability to set aside a solid chunk of time to concentrate and work. The day is so broken up, it seems like there is only five minutes available at one time to actually get work done. Instead of talking about it, we must get focused, set up time for uninterrupted work, and then get that work done.

If you feel like you can only concentrate for very short pieces of time, start there. Assign yourself a task and then work for 45 minutes, giving yourself 15 minutes of each hour to check e-mail, grab a coffee, or touch base with your team. After several days of this discipline, start increasing your time so that are working for 50 minutes, then an hour, and then an hour and fifteen minutes. You'll be amazed at how much you can accomplish when you buckle down and really get into it!

Confidence is not just about how you feel; it affects how you look. When you think about your brand, and the promotion of it within your career, you need to be confident. Just thinking about your personal brand and the impact that you can have on your life is a sign of confidence.

Can we project self-confidence even when we don't feel self-confident? Yes, there are several techniques that you can apply in order to gain confidence.

Pretend You're Confident

Imagine yourself to be a confident person. Get that image in your mind and act it out. Stand up straight, dress better, and try to play the part. If you visualize yourself as confident and successful, that will help you to do things confidently and achieve success. When you feel your confidence slipping, visualize and use positive words to build yourself up.

When Your Positive Self-Talk Doesn't Listen

Sometimes we can be so hard on ourselves that we will actually argue with that voice in our head and therefore can't get the positive message track to enter our consciousness. One helpful way of breaking this pattern is to interfere with it. When you catch yourself listening to negative self-talk, play music that inspires you and sing or hum along. It is much more difficult for those negative messages to persist through music. The music can also be the positive message that you need at that time.

Make Eye Contact

Confident people look people in the eye; people who aren't confident don't, unless it is a cultural restriction. Don't stare or make people uncomfortable; find that comfortable level of engaging in eye contact. (In some cultures, it can be considered rude to look people directly in the eye. Make sure that you know your audience.)

Know Your Stuff

Your confidence can't be all a front. While you are looking people directly in the eyes, standing straight, and otherwise acting as if the world were your oyster, you also have to know what you are doing. If you are prepared and sure of your facts, you've got a better chance of projecting confidence.

Rehearse

Rehearsing can be as simple as writing out a speech or your intended conversation with someone and practicing it in front of the mirror. For example, you could do a role-play with a trusted friend or colleague as the interviewer before you interview for a new position. To tackle your underlying fear of failure, include imagery with your rehearsal: imagine yourself succeeding.

Pep Talks Work

Rather than dwell on the things that didn't work or the things that didn't go well, focus on what you did accomplish. Give yourself a mental pep talk at the beginning or the end of every day. Remind yourself that you have done some things well.

Read Inspiring Biographies and Autobiographies

Build a file of stories that inspire you most. Remember that our capacity far exceeds our usual level of performance. Accept the fact you will have ups and downs just like everyone else. Experiencing them through reading will help reinforce that concept.

Be Thankful

No matter how bad your circumstances, there is probably somebody worse off than you. As well, build excellent support around you. There are a lot of tremendous people out there to spend your valuable time with. However, relationships are fragile. You must be prepared to devote some time to them.

Push Yourself to Accomplish Short-Term Goals

There is no greater way to build confidence than to get things done. Push yourself to get at least three things accomplished each week that move you closer to your goals. Develop a habit of getting things done and being productive.

Do Something for Yourself Every Week

You deserve it. Find a way to celebrate what you have accomplished or overcome. Give yourself some kind of tangible reward for your efforts.

Setting Goals

What Do You Want?

If you really don't know what you want, it's hard to represent your brand and have the impact that you want. Many times, people are looking for the easiest route they can find. As an example, they ask for money in the belief that if we have all the money we could possibly want, everything else would be ours for the taking. However, we all know that isn't exactly how it works. Money doesn't buy happiness, although it does make the search a little easier.

One of life's fundamental truths is, "Ask and you shall receive." Kids can ask for what they want, whether it's an ice cream cone or a new toy. As adults, we seem to lose our ability to ask for what we want, and we can really struggle when it comes to asking for or accepting help. Remember, the world responds to those who ask! There are many different asking strategies. We can create abundance in our lives just by mastering the art of asking assertively.

There are three reasons why we don't ask for what we want.
We believe that it's not right to ask.
We lack confidence.
We fear rejection.

Some people don't enjoy the rewards of asking because they don't ask effectively. Here are five ways to ensure that you get results when you ask.

Ask Clearly

Be precise. Think about your request. Take time to prepare; maybe even write out what you want and practice. Words are powerful so choose them carefully.

Ask with Confidence

You are more apt to get what you want if you speak up and sound confident, rather than hesitant and unsure of yourself. The worst that can happen is that you will be denied, but it probably won't put you in a worse situation than before. If this route is closed, look for another.

Ask Creatively

What can you do to make sure you make an impact and to make certain your request doesn't get lost in the crowd? How could you make your request stand out? How can you make your request fun? Schedule some time every month to dream up new and different ways to ask for what you want.

Ask Sincerely

When you really want help, people will respond. Be willing to be vulnerable. Tell it the way it is, lumps and all. Don't worry if your presentation isn't perfect; ask from your heart.

Help Others

We live in a world of reciprocal relationships and energy. When you give, you get. When you are ready to lend someone a hand, do so. The more you can help others, the more likely that someone will be available to help you when you need it. Be giving of your time, and accepting of theirs.

Identifying Dreams and Setting Goals

Part of the reason people struggle with where they want to go in life is that their goals are vague and ill defined. "More confidence" and "more money" sound really good, but unless we get really clear about what they mean, we may never reach those goals.

Identifying Your Dreams

It is important to give some thought to what we want and how we are going to get there. Right now, we're going to take some time to think about our own hopes and dreams. From that, we will set some concrete goals.

What area(s) of life do you want to set goals in? Some ideas:

- Career (responsibilities or a specific position, or maybe even your own business)
- Income
- Relationships (marriage, children, family, friends, colleagues, customers)
- Things to learn
- Hobbies to take up
- Volunteer activities or charities to support
- Recreational activities
- Home, vehicles, or other possessions to purchase
- Places to travel to
- Spiritual
- Health (examples: lose 20 pounds, exercise more frequently)
- Educational
- Behaviors and habits to develop or change

Now, clearly some of these are achievable in the short term while others will take longer. Some will obviously take more work than others.

SPIRIT

If the goal is quite large, it needs to be broken down into several small, achievable goals that will help you get where you want to go. Good goals should have SPIRIT!

Specific

Be specific about what you want or don't want to achieve. The result should be tangible and measurable. "Talk to people" is pretty ambiguous; "Talk with two of my co-workers each day" is specific.

Prizes

Reward yourself at different points in the goal, particularly if it's long-term. If your goal is to set up a meeting with a new colleague, for example, you might purchase a special treat for yourself afterward.

Individual

The goal must be something that you want to do. If your spouse wants you to lose 20 pounds but you think you look fine, you're not going to want to work towards the goal.

Review

Review your progress periodically. Does the goal still make sense to you? Is it still giving you energy and something you find motivating? Are you stuck? Do you need to adjust certain parts of it?

Inspiring

Frame the goal positively. Make it fun to accomplish. You could make a poster of the end result, frame it, and post it on the wall.

Time-Bound

Give yourself a deadline for achieving the goal. Even better, split the goal into small parts and give yourself a deadline for each item.

Getting Some SPIRIT Template
Goal Statement

_____

_____

_____

_____

Check to make sure you have included each of these elements.

Specific	
Prizes	
Individual	
Review	
Inspiring	

Who will you check in with?

_____

_____

_____

_____

When are your check-in dates? What should be accomplished by each one?

Date	Task

Being Flexible and Resilient

When you are setting up big goals (which can include this shift you are making in having personal impact and creating your personal brand), there's a very good chance you will hit some setbacks. People you thought would be supportive may not be. You may let your guard down and have your brand tarnished. Your ability to bounce back after these setbacks is essential in reaching your goals. Being able to apply some flexibility and resilience is a way to measure how successful – and happy – you are.

Some people may appear to be more resilient than others. While this ability may be innate for some, a lot of the behaviors are learned. The evidence of learning means that we can all develop traits of resilience and flexibility. We have organized our top five tips as the 5 D's.

Develop a Positive Self-Concept

Resilient people know that they are worth it and they see themselves in a positive way. A positive self-concept does not mean you have to behave like someone who is self-centered or selfish. It does mean that you perceive yourself in a positive way.

Develop Relationships

Resilient people tend to give to and be a part of strong networks. Friends, family, business partnerships, and colleagues are all a source of support when things are not going well. Accountability partners can help get things back on track.

Develop Appreciation

Focusing on things that are going well helps bring more good things into view. This will help you to regain a positive mindset if you have let go of it. It also helps you to deal with challenges more effectively than if you are focusing on what's going wrong.

Develop Acceptance

No matter how positive, flexible, and resilient you are, there are things that cannot be changed. Resilient people accept these things, instead of spending precious energy fighting things that cannot be altered.

Develop Vision

When you look at your life, your goals, and your business from a distance, problems and setbacks seem less important than when they are close up. Develop your vision and then focus on the ability to call it up whenever you wish.

Networking for Success

Networking is an effective way for you to build your brand. However, building a network can be a difficult thing for a lot of people. If you are inhibited at all, the idea of introducing yourself to people can be daunting. If you are outgoing, people may have the impression you just want to meet them to further your career or grow your business. The real purpose of networking, however, is that you bring something to the group that is helpful to them (not you specifically) without expecting something directly in return.

For example, if you know someone who needs their house painted, and you know a painter, you could introduce the two. You do not gain directly from the referral, except that now it's possible that the person you refer and the painter will both think of you when they have a need or a referral for you.

There are plenty of networking groups available to help you get out into your community and to get known. Building a network takes time and patience. If you are hoping to get business or recognition from a group, expect it to take a year or more. Your results will depend on how involved you are.

Here are some excellent tips to try as you start to build or expand upon your network:

- If you are a strong writer or teacher, you can write for a variety of media (such as local news, websites, and blogs). Just make sure your work is getting read and that it's work you are proud of.
- If you enjoy presentations, then volunteer to sit on a panel or start looking for paid workshops and conference presentations.
- Get away from time wasters, such as water cooler gossip, or people who socialize excessively at work and are not getting things done. You don't want to be associated with these people because they will not be a good reflection of your brand.
- Spend time with mentors and coaches in the workplace that you can learn from, even if it's just while sharing a meal or break together now and again.

Building Your Credibility

We've probably all worked with people (including leaders) that we did not respect. No matter how long we worked with them, and no matter how great our results were, there was something about them which stopped us from trusting them. This lack of respect leads to dysfunctional teams, where people are afraid of repercussions. When people work well with one another, and respect one another, trust is built.

Factors that impact your credibility include small things (like remembering to think of people and send a thank you note) and big things (like being punctual). Credibility is affected by your ability to engender trust. It is reinforced when people speak about you in a manner that reflects the regard they hold you in.

Below are five ways that you can develop trusting relationships.

If you say you'll do it, then get on and do it.

Some people are good at planning and setting things up, but not so good when it comes to the follow through. At some point, you have to stop talking and start doing. If details are not really your strong suit, then make sure that you have people you can delegate to so that the things you say you will do get done. If you break promises, any trust that people have in you will be swiftly eroded.

If you mess it up, own it.

We all make mistakes, and it's a way to learn how to improve. Instead of pointing the finger at someone else (especially members of your team), make sure the blame falls where it belongs – on you. Leaders and people who want to have impact learn that accepting responsibility for the good and the bad builds trust and credibility.

Be there for people.

If people feel micro-managed, they feel that you do not trust them to do their own work. Allow them to experiment, take risks, and to learn from failure as well as their own choices. Remember to also see what their strengths are and to celebrate when they do things well. Don't try to take credit when the whole team is contributing to success. As well, make sure that you are available when they need your support through mentoring and coaching.

Be assertive.

Although this is something that varies culturally and even within industries, you've got to be prepared to stand up for the things you believe in. You must also develop tools to manage conflict and to solve problems. If everyone that you work with seems accepting of everything you do and say, chances are that they are afraid of telling you the truth about how they really feel. Encourage sharing of opinions, debate, and discussion as a way for everyone to learn and grow.

Be yourself.

Demonstrating your brand and having a personal impact on the things that you do does not mean that you become someone else in public. Be accepting of who you are (including your strengths and weaknesses) and commit to ongoing development so that you can be the best person you can be.

Defining Your Brand

When we refer to your brand, we're thinking about the package that you want to offer to others. This is a small-scale version of a corporate brand, and vastly different from a cattle brand. Thinking about your personal brand can seem a bit vague, so let's make it something that is more tangible.

When a company considers their brand, they do so in terms of **standards**. Their logo will be created, and with that will be rules (standards) about how the logo is placed on a page, whether it can be reproduced in black and white or must always be in color, what uniforms staff need to wear, how the business itself will be presented, and so on.

Your brand is not the same as a corporate brand, but it has some similar elements. **Your brand** is a reflection of the story that you want to tell about yourself and how you wish for others to see you. Over time, as you evolve as a human being (and as you age), your story changes. You finish some things, you start others, and things that are important at one stage of your life may lose importance over time. Your goals will also change over time.

If you think of what you want said of you in the public, those things would be a good representation of your brand, wouldn't they? The best exercise for this is to think about what will be said about you when you can no longer speak for yourself, when you have passed away and someone is writing a eulogy in tribute to you or writing an obituary.

Managing Your Social Media Presence

You need to develop a curiosity about how people see you online and what is said about you. This can be managed by putting your own name in search engines and by taking good care of popular social networking sites such as LinkedIn, Facebook, and Twitter.

Learn to set up automatic searches for your name (such as through a Google Alert), so that you will receive an e-mail that lets you know your name has been mentioned online. Make sure that pictures, comments, e-mail signatures, and articles that are about you support your brand. If they do not support your brand, make sure you have them removed so that they don't detract from the impact you are aiming for.

When your presence in person and online is well managed, you have the opportunity to exert influence without anyone observing that you are being incongruent with your brand. This means that you can have the impact that you desire, without concern that something from your past might come forward to derail your efforts.

Social media is an evolving and influential medium for sharing information. If you say something that someone notices, and they click on a "share" button, your message can be spread throughout an increasing number of sites that include blogs, wikis, forums, podcasts, photo sites, and bookmarks. Social media has been created specifically to share information among networks, and its popularity continues to grow. Leveraging social media is an incredible way for a single message to be spread, but the downside is that a message that you later want to recant can be very hard to get rid of.

This means that if you make comments about somebody that you dislike, a company that you want to complain about, a book that struck a nerve, or an opinion about something going on in politics, you've got to keep in mind that those comments can be tracked back to you. You must be mindful about what you place online.

When it comes to getting a promotion, applying for a new job, or trying to secure a contract, Human Resources departments and your contacts regularly search the Internet to see what is there. In order to maintain the integrity of your brand, you need to do the same. Search for your name (and all variations of it, including images) in several different search engines and see what appears. Do these messages support your brand? Do they tarnish your image in any way? Make sure that anything that does not represent who you are is properly removed.

In order to manage your presence on social media, we recommend that you reserve your name on any social networking site that you come across so that other people cannot pretend to be you. Then, create a consistent message (your brand) across all sites that you use. Don't think that you have to be active on every site, because you don't. Spend as little time as you can on just a couple of sites, and save the rest of your time for achieving your goals.

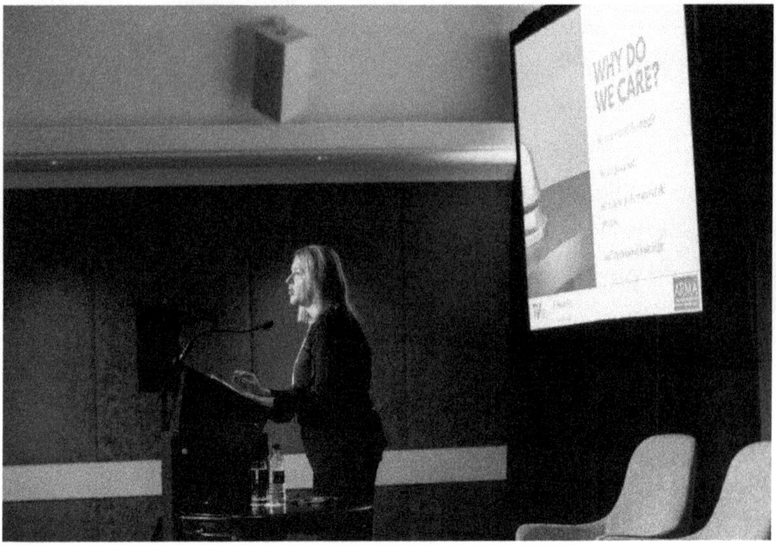
WHY DO
WE CARE?

CHAPTER 8

PRESENTATION ESSENTIALS

"Sometimes you find out the things you are supposed to be doing, by doing the things you are not supposed to do" – Oprah Winfrey

Presentations, whether in person or via video interface, remain a primary means of building business relationships and partnerships that will sustain and grow your company. In the filled calendars of busy customers and investors, time is literally money. In 10-Minute Presentations, you will learn how to craft and polish an engaging, professional presentation that shares your message and call to action swiftly and clearly. This will maximize your impact, conversions and productivity.

Presentations and Relationships

This is a course about presentations. It is also a course about relationships. Every contact made, professionally or personally, is a potential relationship. Whether a relationship develops depends on the mutual interests and desires of those involved.

A 10-minute presentation gives you and your audience 600 seconds to share, learn, and choose action, to decide whether to shift from contact to relationship, or to say 'thanks but no thanks.'

What a Presenter Wants

A presentation expresses your interests and desires in a way that enables your audience to make informed, timely decisions. An effective presentation on your part supports action that you desire on their part.

As a presenter, you want:
- Undivided attention
- Interest
- Motivation
- Action

To gain all of these things, your presentation needs to be relevant — connecting to a topic, problem, or challenge to which your audience can relate. Your presentation needs to answer their questions before they ask, keep them interested, gain their trust and then gain their support. As a presenter you want to leave the room knowing you have made an impact and gained an ally.

Reflect: Presenter
Consider a recent presentation you have given and answer the following questions.

1. What were your goals and were they achieved?

2. How was the experience — positive or negative? Why?

What an Audience Wants

Consider the saying: "You never get a second chance to make a first impression."

In many cases, presentations are the first impression you get to make to a prospective client, funder, partner, or buyer. In other cases, presentations are the follow-up, a deal sealer or, (although hopefully not) a deal breaker. In any case, you will be giving your presentation to people who are busy, impatient, and want clear information now so they can make an informed decision sooner rather than later.

An audience wants:

- To feel valued
- To be heard
- To see themselves in what is being presented
- To be entertained
- A clear ask
- A clear path to next steps
- And they want all of this in a few blinks of the eye.

Reflect: Audience
Consider a recent presentation you have received.

1. How was the experience — positive or negative? Why?

2. Were you motivated to action? Why or why not?

The Common Ground

The lists of goals for presenters and audiences seem extensive on either side, and impossible to accomplish in only 10 minutes.

However, there may be more common ground than you think.

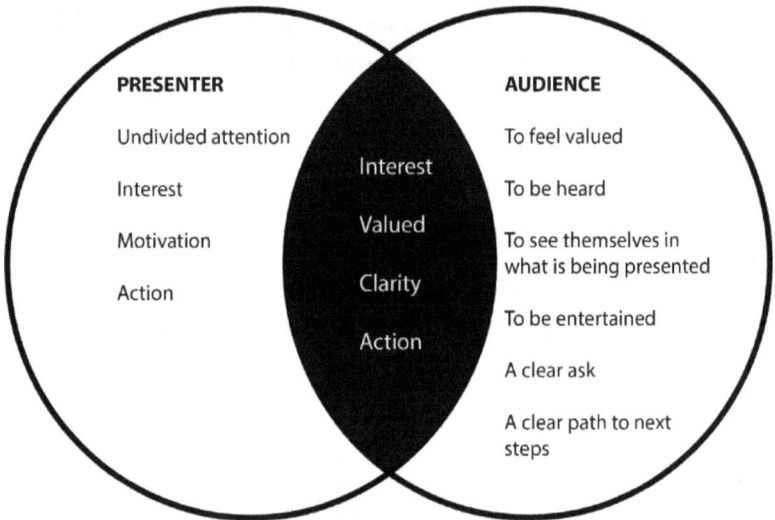

PRESENTER

Undivided attention

Interest

Motivation

Action

Interest

Valued

Clarity

Action

AUDIENCE

To feel valued

To be heard

To see themselves in what is being presented

To be entertained

A clear ask

A clear path to next steps

Choosing the Platform

Real or Virtual?

Choose according to your resources, experience, comfort level and audience needs.

In other words, choose the option in which everyone will get the most positive experience possible.

Some tools of the trade
Here are just a few examples of downloadable or online tools that can be used for both face-to-face and online presentations.

PowerPoint, Google Slides and Keynote

These platforms can be used to create slide shows that support your presentations. PowerPoint is a Microsoft product; Google Slides is part of the online Google Docs suite and Keynote is found on Apple devices. Note the use of the word **support.** Too often, these programs are used as scripts, when they should be used as prompts.

You audience wants to listen to you. As a presenter, you want to make the most of the brief time you have to interact with your viewers. If they just wanted to read, or be read to, they would download a file. They want the human interaction, and so do you. Slides should be simple highlights of what you are presenting or discussing. We will discuss this further in the coming sessions.
https://products.office.com/

Canva

Canva is an online tool used to create graphics – combining photos, text, shapes and backgrounds into effective visuals that can enhance your presentations, or be used as promotional tools (posters, social media posts, for example) to promote your presentations.
There is a free option and a paid premium option:
https://www.canva.com/

Video scribe

This is a virtual white board that you can use as you would use a physical white board with markers, allowing you to take instant notes, highlight questions or draw diagrams for your physical or virtual audiences.
https://www.videoscribe.co/en

Your Personal Toolbox

The software and virtual tools just discussed are important supports for any presentation, but there are two tools only you can provide. Whether your venue is physical or virtual, you will always need these two tools to be at the ready and used appropriately.

These tools are your face and your voice.

Whether in person or via a screen, communication between humans is the same. We share information verbally with our words and nonverbally with our facial expressions, body language and tone of voice. In fact, some studies say more than half of the message we receive is determined by facial expression and body language. That is why visuals – such as video, webinars and in-person presentations – are such powerful tools for attracting attention and building relationships. And that is why there are some guidelines for giving solid presentations that work equally well for either an online delivery system or a conference room.

These guidelines are:

Keep your face visible.

Eye contact is a universal sign of respect, that you care about your audience and are confident in what you are sharing with them. Looking down at your notes too much, turning your back on your audience to read from your slides, or filling their lines of sight with graphics and videos is rude at best, and alienating at worst.

This is of particular importance for online presentations: the audience knows you cannot see them, so they have no problem leaving during what they feel is a 'boring part' to grab a snack, get a drink or check their newsfeeds. But physical audiences will show their disengagement as well, by pulling out their phones, chatting with their neighbors or leaving. You only have 10 minutes, but you can lose an audience in a minute if they feel you do not value their presence, or yours, enough to engage eye to eye.

Use all of your voice … or at least a good range of it.

Our voices offer an orchestra of sounds: tones, inflections, pauses, intensity. These variations add dimension and shading to your words, as layers of color add depth and mood to a drawing. Your audience is not seeking facts and figures;

they are seeking to connect with you and your message, and for you to connect with them. You can do that across the stage or the screen by how or when you speak.

Reading in a monotone tells them that you are not connecting with anything other than the script you prepared before even meeting them. However, a voice that is piercing, high-pitched and shrill with contrived enthusiasm is the equivalent of a fire alarm – nothing will empty your room faster. Aim for even relaxed tones punctuated with small bursts of energy to make a point or lift the mood. Listen to expert presenters and notice how they use inflections to strengthen their message.

Use your voice to create silence.

That is correct. Use your voice by not using your voice. Pauses serve two purposes:

- Accentuate a point
- Invite interactions, like questions or discussion

Both of these types of pauses keep your presentation interesting and your audience engaged. Just be sure to now make them too long. Then it becomes an awkward pause, where your audience becomes confused, concerned for your well-being or otherwise loses focus. Make sure your pause is well-timed and your eye contact and facial expressions remain engaging.

We have examined tools of the trade and venue options. Now, let's start creating a presentation that makes the best use of your tools, your venue options and the 10 minutes you have promised your audience.

Outlining your Presentation

With your theme in place and your takeaways now clear, outline your presentation topic by topic, slide by slide. A general outline could look like this:

Introduction

- Who you are: name, job title, role with the company
- Why you are speaking with them today
- Title of your presentation
- What you will discuss
- What they will take away

Theme

- Problem/Issue
- How things started
- Situation today
- Need for action
- Why you/your organization is best positioned to act

Action/Solution

- What is needed
- Why audience should care
- What audience can do

Summary

- Key points revisited
- Action revisited

- Thanks
- Contact information

Drafting Your Presentation

The outline is the skeleton of your presentation, the essential information you need to share. Now is the time to add narrative and visuals to flesh out and clothe the skeleton, creating a presentation that will engage your audience and encourage them to act.

Checklist for Creation

- Will the presentation be in-person or virtual?
- If virtual, what platform will be used?
- What is the theme of your presentation?
- What are the takeaways?

Are all of these elements included or reflected in your outline?

Slides and Visuals

Investor and author Guy Kawasaki developed 10-20-30, a simple mantra for creating slide show presentations: 10 slides, 20 minutes, font at least 30 points or larger.

A few years later, Astrid Klein and Mark Dytham created PechaKucha, a Japanese form of electronic storytelling that offers 20 slides with 20 seconds of narrative per slide.

These are but two examples of presentations designed to provide information in a short, engaging, and focused way.

Too few slides or not enough information can make the presentation slow and boring; too many can be overwhelming and cause your message to be lost or forgotten.

If you imagine a 10-minute presentation as a series of slides, there would be a maximum of one minute – 60 seconds – per slide. This can be a starting point for organizing and focusing information.

What is the one key point you would include on each page?

Creating Visuals

Visuals can be a faster way than words alone to share or reinforce important pieces of your presentation. Visuals can include slides, photos, videos, graphs, charts, and strategic use of color in text: headlines, underlining, and highlighting. Here are a few guidelines to creating and using effective visuals in your presentation:

Keep it Simple

- No to Animations, Yes to high-quality graphics
- Limit transitions and animations
- Embrace white space – no more than one headline or phrase on a page
- Include video or audio where appropriate, but avoid sound effects and gimmicks: let your content speak for itself

Show vs. Tell

Use charts or graphs where possible

Avoid scripting – include keywords only on your visuals, not your entire text

Video or audio can keep things interesting, give real-life testimonials or shot that puts the person 'right there'

Appearance is Everything

- Color can attract, engage, and invite support or action
- Cool colors (blue and green) work for backgrounds
- Warm colors (orange and red) work for text
- A popular color scheme is a blue background with white text
- In bright light, a white or light background with black or dark text is highly visible
- Choose fonts that are sans serif, such as Arial or Calibri (like the text you are reading right now.) Sans serif tends to be clear and clean in all resolutions and situations

Preparing to Present

The presentation is one of three parts to the overall presentation experience.

The other two parts:

You as presenter

The equipment and technology connecting you and your audience

You as Presenter

You have had instruction and created a checklist to be a peer reviewer.

This can help guide you as a presenter on what to do and what not to do.

As mentioned, speaking in public or in front of an audience is not always a natural skill. There can be discomfort involved, even fear. If acknowledged and controlled, that fear can be translated into energy that makes your presentation more vibrant and the best it can be. Avoiding the fear can result in your presentation being subdued as you follow a rehearsed script or engage timidly to avoid making a mistake. The key to turning fear into a tool is turning negative thoughts into positive energy.

Regardless of how well planned and delivered presentations are, there will always be mistakes, surprises and audiences that do not respond. When these things happen, it is important to use them as learning experiences rather than weapons to attack your self-esteem or abilities.

The 'What-Ifs'

It is also important to realize that fear lives in the unknown. In some cases, the nervousness that threatens your ability to deliver a confident presentation grows from imagined problems, the 'what-ifs.' 'What if the power goes out?' 'What if no one laughs at the opening joke?' 'What if I need to sneeze during the podcast?' The 'what-ifs' can be endless and unrelenting. Worst of all, the what-ifs consumer energy and concentration that could be used to strengthen your presentation. One way to deal with the 'what-ifs' is the beat them at their own game.

For example, Geoffrey James listed eight habits that can ruin presentations. Read about them here:

https://www.dalecarnegie.co.uk/8-habits-that-ruin-good-presentations/

Dealing with some of these habits in advance can answer the 'what-ifs' with an action plan. Answering the 'if' with a 'then' directs energy from churning inward to flowing outward.

For example:

'What if the laptop for my slide show does not work?'

Answer it with:

'Then make sure you have a paper copy that you can refer to during the presentation.'

'What if my presentation starts to run too long?'

Answer it with:

'Then honor the promise you made to your audience. Wrap things up quickly and end at the scheduled time. If you have not covered anything, end with a reference to the website or email where they can get more information.'

"What if I am asked a question and I do not know the answer?'

Answer it with:

'Then be polite and helpful. Thank them for the question, offer any information you have that might help and ask to see them after the presentation, or to give you a contact email or phone number, so you can continue the conversation after you have checked into their inquiry.'

Appearing Professional

As mentioned in Session Two: *You never get a second chance to make a first impression.*

In this multimedia world, you have seconds to make that impression.

Whether appearing in person or online, it is important to dress and act in a way that will inspire confidence in your abilities and encourage people to both listen to what you say, and take it seriously. Your grooming and clothing should reflect who you are and speak to the audience with whom you wish to engage. Whatever style best fits for your presentation, it must be authentic. Pretending to be someone else or representing something that you do not represent could insult your audience and erode your credibility. As with your presentation content, avoid gimmicks. Let your knowledge and abilities speak for themselves.

A large part of your appearance is body language, how you move and act.

Nervousness can result in habits that may be distracting or uncomfortable for your audience to watch. Be mindful of these common distractions, and what to do about them:

Fidgeting:

Rustling or shifting papers, tapping your pen on the table, playing with your necklace, pacing … you may do any or all of these without noticing but after a minute or two, this is all your audience will see. The next step for them is to make it stop by tuning out mentally or leaving altogether. Try speaking in front of a mirror to see if there are any repetitive, unnecessary movements. Plan where your papers will be, where you will place your hands, and where you will stand. Breathe with each movement.

Eye Contact:

We have discussed the importance of eye contact, which is necessary to engage your audience. During an in-person presentation, ensure eye contact is in the form of steady glances at people seated throughout the room. No one person wants to be stared at or repeatedly singled out, nor do the others want to feel left out. In a virtual presentation, 'eye' contact is between you and the camera. Again, vary this to ensure your audience does not feel uncomfortable, but also ensure you repeat eye contact with the camera lens every few seconds. Glancing down at notes, over at a visual or away as you contemplate a question keeps things interesting. Staring down for more than 10 seconds or turning your back to the camera (or on the audience if in person) as you search for something or read from your slides breaks your connection with the audience. It could also be perceived as rude.

Relaxed vs Rigid:

A relaxed demeanour can exude confidence. It can also seem sloppy or uncaring.

A straight upright posture can be inspiring, or it can be boring to watch.

It is important to find your comfort zone, then observe yourself in a mirror or on video to see how that looks. Peer review can also help with this. A slight straightening or relaxing of your spine might make things more comfortable for you and your audience.

Also be mindful of the pace of your speech. If you are a naturally fast talker, then ensure the excitement or nerves of presenting do not speed up your speech beyond what the ear and brain can comfortably process. Be mindful as well that speaking too slowly will reduce the information you can share in 10 minutes, and may also lower the attention span of your audience.

VIDEO

Today there are many tools on the market that can help anyone create professional looking videos in minutes and thanks to the advancement of technology all of us can film high quality videos on our phones in seconds. You will have noticed the explosion of selfie videos across social media platforms. Video is so successful because it is interesting and engaging content that can be quickly and easily consumed and can convey powerful messages through voice/text and images. With the addition of background music, you can tap into many of the senses and leave an audience feeling uplifted and inspired.

YouTube has also become a powerful and accessible marketing channel for many business owners. Providing powerful content with links through to product pages is a great and inexpensive way to promote your products and services. Video is also a fast and powerful way to gain a profile and a following and build your brand and image.

Video can be used as part of the marketing strategy for your business, is a great way to quickly demonstrate and teach a particular topic or set of instructions and also adds interest and excitement to your presentations.

You can even use video to welcome new clients to your business or have clients submit video testimonials on your products and services, which are more powerful than just plain text.

If you are speaking to camera to introduce a product or service it is really important to use the "Who, What, Why, How" script. You often only have a few seconds to grab their attention so focus on who you are, what do you have them, why should they care or take action and how can they take action.

Practice so you sound natural and non-scripted, dress appropriately for the occasion and remember to pause, breathe and look straight into the camera and imagine you are speaking directly to a familiar face and close friend or colleague.

BONUS TIPS FROM MELISSA

The minutes leading up to a presentation can feel super-intense. When your heart's beating so fast, it feels like it's going to jump right out of your chest.

Presenting is a big part of business, whether it's presenting your course material, webinars, Facebook lives, client presentations or keynote speeches at conferences and virtual events.

It's easy to think that a virtual presentation is less stressful because your audience is not physically in front of you. At least that's what I thought initially, however, I was wrong. It offers a whole set of different challenges where preparation and practice are still key, just like any presentation, but raises its own set of challenges, most notably, you can't read your audience.

If presenting to camera conjures up feelings of extreme panic then we will walk through everything I've learnt about what you need to do before, during and after your virtual presentation, so you have a proven action plan for success.

I had built up years of face-to-face training, speaking at live events and moderating panel sessions, where presenting started to feel easier and dare I say it, actually enjoyable! But transitioning to presenting on camera was a whole new thing. When I first started, I would constantly look down at my notes and totally forget that I needed to look into the camera to make eye contact with my audience.

Prepare

1. Think about your stage

You don't need an expensive studio setup to create a super professionally lit video, whether you're using natural light from a window or you invest a small amount into a ring light (you can get these for $50 or less on Amazon!).
Just make sure the light is in front of your face, rather than behind you to avoid looking dark on screen.

A space in your home is all you need and if it has lots of natural light, even better. The trick is to keep it simple and make sure it is quiet and **no background noise.**
If you decide to use a virtual background, you could buy a portable green screen. Or for an easy DIY green screen, just buy a piece of material and stick it on the wall behind you... and *voila...* your very own gorgeous green screen.

When presenting it feels natural to stand (as you would in real life) which means you can use your whole body to express yourself. If this is too hard with your set-up you can of course present from sitting down.

Just make sure you feel as comfortable and natural as possible, and adjust your monitor to ensure your face is well centered in the camera view (if using your desktop camera) so as you don't have half of your head cut off!
Find a comfortable posture and try not to move around too much so you stay in frame. A good posture exudes confidence.

Be natural with your hand movements and do not over do them, you want to have energy in your presentation through your voice and actions but not over-exaggerate so it appears un-natural and a distraction.

2. Plan and Practice

How well you prepare yourself and how often you practice will make an enormous difference. It will also ensure you can handle any last-minute curve balls that may occur without appearing rattled.

Make notes on everything you want to say, I always write out a word-for-word script alongside the appropriate slide if I am using a slide-deck presentation. I tend to print it out and hand-write my notes on, but you can also type your notes into your presentation.

If you have a camera on you whilst presenting your main key points you need to factor in that you don't want to look like you are reading notes either, maintaining eye contact with your audience by looking into the camera is important. You can place key dot points of your main discussion points on paper on the walls behind your camera and laptop or off to the side, so whilst you are actually glancing sideways to look at your next points, it appears you are just "in thought".

Another trick is to have the video camera on at the start and the end, however, when you get into the main part of your presentation you can switch of the camera and just have voice to slide. This is very powerful for the audience because it allows them to focus on the content on your slide and your important messages in your voice and reduces the temptation and distraction of them focusing on your video thumbnail and checking out your background, and you and what you are wearing etc.

It also allows you to then read from your notes, reducing the stress of memorising your content and accidently missing a key point, however, be sure to make it sound like you are not reading and it is very natural.

This tip works especially well for webinars and online training sessions, however, if you are doing a keynote then often the camera is required to be left on. You can also set up a second screen with your notes behind the main camera and if you stand back a bit, the audience can't tell when you are not exactly looking directly at the camera.

Today I often use a teleprompter which means I have my entire word-for-word script scrolling in front of me. There are commercial options, however, there are also very easy home-made teleprompter options as well. I recommend doing an online search and you find them!

What to wear?

Ideally stick to solid colours and limit too many patterns. You want to be comfortable but you also have to think about your background and how you look against it.

Remember to dress for your audience and the occasion. Just because you may be working more from home or presenting from home, doesn't mean you can always rock up in your casual gear…although you can often have your slippers on under the table! I ran a two day online virtual summit from my home office with my Ugg boots on under the table – my feet have never felt so good at a conference!

You don't want to be fidgeting with your clothes while you are presenting which will be distracting for your audience, and you also have to think about how a lapel microphone and its battery pack can be attached to your clothing.

This is especially important for stand-up live events. I ran one live conference and my keynote speaker looked fabulous in a slim fitting black dress, however, there was no belt or pocket to attach the battery pack of the microphone to and know collar for a lapel to clip easily too.

The expert AV team quickly attached the battery pack down the back of her dress to her bra strap! She totally rocked the presentation, however, revealed after she was so nervous her bra strap may have unclipped mid presentation and had the battery pack drop out from under her dress live on stage! Thankfully this did not happen and now makes for a great story, however, it brings home the point.

If presenting on camera also make sure you have you make-up on hand for quick touch-ups. Somehow shiny looks all the shinier on camera.
Practice does make perfect. There's no way around this one. You have to keep practicing and the same applies for live in-person events as well.

Do a test run (or two) of the whole virtual presentation from start to finish, with everything set up as it would be on the actual day.

Practice what you are going to say as many times as you can, and say it out a loud, not just in your head. This really does help!

Each time you run through it, you will feel more confident and as you gain experience, you won't need to practice as many times to feel ready.

The better you know your content, the less you'll have to refer to your notes and the more easily you can incorporate bonus content and stories, or engage with the audience and not feel derailed, you can even cope with a tech glitch more confidently as well without losing your train of thought.

An additional tip is to always be prepared to have to present your content without a slide-deck just in-case there is a technical glitch on the day or even part way through your presentation.

3. Test everything

Your goal is to get to a point where you are totally comfortable with all the tech you are using, e.g. how to switch the camera on and off, how to mute and unmute, how to show slides, where to read comments, how to respond to and acknowledge chat box messages, how to grant additional access to attendees if needed and how to record – make sure you don't forget to do this!

I know that moment when you say something so profound on a live webinar and then realize you were on mute the whole time! Or had not hit the record button.

There will come a point that it's second nature to you, but test and test again.

Don't forget to also check your internet speed and boost it if needed. The faster, the better! The faster and more stable your internet connection, the clearer your audio and visual will be, and plugging directly into your modem will give you the strongest signal.

Or if you have to use WIFI and are at home, make sure the bandwidth is not being drained by Netflix.

Technology can be stressful and as someone that also runs events both virtual and in-person the technology is so crucial to the success of your event that it remains one of the biggest areas of stress.

I ran a two-day virtual summit in 2020 with 50 speakers and hundreds of delegates and 2 days later the internet provider company had a major system outage right across Sydney! Thank goodness that did not impact my event. It is important to plan for all sorts of situations and ensure you have a back up for internet and even a back-up laptop should yours decide to not work the morning of your event!

Make sure you check your sound. Good sound makes a world of difference and can make or break your event.

You have something to say and people need to hear it.

I'm not talking about buying an expensive boom microphone, in fact, even the microphone on those free headphones that come with your mobile phone are better than nothing!

As long as you make sure that your sound is clear so they can hear you from start to finish.

This means testing all your equipment and your internet connection beforehand. You don't want to lose viewers because they can't hear you properly. It is also really upsetting when you have recorded a fantastic live session and when you play back the recording the sound quality is really poor.

When you are live

1. Engage your audience

It's a bit more challenging to engage virtually because you can't see your audience, but it's not totally impossible. What can be difficult is you can't read your audience if you are presenting to a large group and they have their cameras off, even if their cameras are on it is difficult to pick up the "vibe" of the room.

Many skilled presenters really draw from the room and their energy and this is very challenging to do so in a virtual presentation.

Be expressive and emotive when you're presenting, and vary the tone of your voice so that your audience doesn't get bored.

Use your body language to show that you are open and comfortable (even if you're not feeling it). You want your audience to know that you are fully invested in giving them your best!

Build in breaks for activities if it suits your presentation and have them come back to you once the work is done. You can also pause and get engagement by running a poll or stopping for some Q&A in the chat box. Be sure you plan all of this in to the timing of your session as you don't want to get stuck answering questions that then cut short your presenting time and you don't get all of your content out.

Be also mindful of other speakers you might be sharing the stage with; you do not want to run over because this will put pressure on the other speakers and cut into their time and also place pressure on the event host as they must run the session to time.

When you stop to read audience comments, mention people's names and acknowledge that you've read what they've said, whether it's answering a question or sharing your opinion about what they've said.

It makes them feel special and important and confirms to them that you are in fact live.

2. Make eye contact

This WILL feel uncomfortable at first when you are staring at a camera and not at an actual face.
But making and keeping eye contact is important to connect with your audience and to hold their attention.
You might be comfortable speaking on stages to thousands, but as soon as that single round camera lens points at your face you freeze. You can also tend to look down at the faces

of your delegates if they are on camera, however, then they see you looking down rather than at them.

But, learning to master this skill will be the difference between producing an amateur and an ultra-professional virtual presentation.

If you keep focus on that lens it will look like you are locking eyes with each individual person watching your visual presentation.

3. Pace yourself

The trick is finding the perfect pace – not so fast that your audience misses half of what you are saying and not too slow that they fall asleep.

Remember to take deep breaths and to pause periodically when it seems natural, but timing is critical – you do not want to run over!

Now that it's over

1. Edit and publish

Video editing can be easily outsourced or done yourself. Two great tools I use are:
Movavi
Animoto
And then I publish on either Vimeo or YouTube

2. Review and improve

Whether it's pre-recorded or live, watching back the virtual presentation is 100% essential.

Even though that can be super uncomfortable, it's the ONLY way to improve!

When you feel like cringing as you watch a recording, you can learn and improve.

You're here to serve your market, and if you can improve one thing about how you present each time, it could increase your impact, your influence and ultimately your revenue.

YOUTUBE.COM
HM Awards 2019

CHAPTER 9

PLAN FOR SUCCESS

"Many people fail in life not because they aim too high and miss, but because they aim to low and hit" – *Les Brown*

Despite our best efforts, we remain in an imperfect and unpredictable world. Even if you prepare, practice, polish and deliver it with enthusiasm, a well-crafted and well-planned presentation may still underperform according to your goals or fail to connect with your audience. Why? Your audience may be distracted by other events or deadlines, the venue or platform may be uncomfortable, Mercury may be in retrograde ... there may be an explanation, or there may be no reason at all. You cannot control audience reaction, but you can control your reaction.

First, let go of remorse, guilt or shame. Negative talk will only ruin your mood and your chance of giving a successful presentation in the future.

Robbie Senbach describes how he learned from his worst presentation.
Read his blog here:
https://robbiesenbach.com/worst-presentation-ever-gave/

Examining Your Presentation

Dr. Michelle Mazur describes a Presentation Autopsy — examining a presentation for clues and suggestions on what to repeat and what to include next time.
See her blog here:
https://drmichellemazur.com/2013/07/what-to-do-if-your-presentation-sucked.html
Some questions to consider:

- Did I leave enough time and head space to prepare?
- Did I know my audience?
- Was I clear with my goal?
- Did I properly understand my subject material?
- Did I practice and polish?
- Did I stay focused in my delivery?

Sometimes our enthusiasm or passion can get the better of us. Then we go off script, sharing our personal stories which can be entertaining yet distracting, especially when people are busy and you have a 10-minute time limit to get to the point. Ensure your presentation has enough room for 'you to be you' without losing the focus of your talk.
As mentioned, a presentation may perform poorly for no definable reason. However, reviewing the steps and examining for opportunities to improve turn any presentation into a positive experience for learning.

Presentation Autopsy

Using the review questions discussed in this section, analyze their presentations and rate your performance for each question on a scale of one to 10: with one being lowest accomplishment and 10 being the best accomplishment.

Make notes with each rating on:
What went well?
What can be improved for the next time?

Did I leave enough time and head space to prepare? Yes ☐ No ☐ Rating 1-10: _____
NOTES:

_____

_____

_____

_____

Did I know my audience? Yes ☐ No ☐ Rating 1-10: _____
NOTES:

_____

_____

_____

_____

Was I clear with my goal? Yes ☐ No ☐ Rating 1-10: _____
NOTES:

_____

_____

_____

Did I properly understand my subject material? Yes ☐ No ☐
Rating 1-10: _____
NOTES:

_____

_____

_____

_____

Did I practice and polish? Yes ☐ No ☐ Rating 1-10: _____
NOTES:

_____

_____

_____

_____

Did I stay focused in my delivery?   Yes ☐ No ☐ Rating
1-10: _____
NOTES:

_____

_____

_____

_____

What went well:

_____

_____

_____

_____

What can be improved for the next time:
1.

_____

PLAN FOR SUCCESS

_____

_____

_____

Further Review Questions

Timing:
- Did it start and finish on time?

Content:
- Was the theme and message clear?
- Did the information given support the theme and message?
- Were visuals and narrative informative and appropriate?

Delivery:
- Did the presenter make eye contact?
- Did the presenter speak clearly?
- Did the presenter demonstrate knowledge of the subject?

Impact:
- Did this presentation inform?
- Did this presentation persuade?
- Do you feel you learned or gained from this presentation?

Lessons Learned

With the results of your autopsy, some additional troubleshooting may help with planning for next time.

Check the Tech
- Electronic and network problems are often unpredictable and beyond our control.

- The best way to cope is focus on what we can control.
- In this case, we can control our dependence on these systems.

Duplicate or Backup

- List the essential elements to your presentation and have an alternate plan for each.
- Have two laptops ready in case one stops working.
- Be able to access two Wi-Fi networks or a backup data account if needed.
- Have your slide show on your computer, on a separate device and on paper.
- Ensure all devices are fully charged.

Time and Test

- Leaving yourself enough time to test the projector, laptop, sound system, internet signal and to become familiar with the buttons, remote controls and speed is the best defence. Also, identify a person or a help number that you can contact if you need assistance.

Light and Sound

Your webinar is perfectly planned, except for the sunlight that suddenly streams through your window and overwhelms your screen. Check windows and coverings. Know where the light switches and control panels are. Also, be mindful of air conditioners, heating systems and air exchangers. If you are exposed to them constantly you may not hear them but your audience will, especially if you need to speak over them or your computer microphone enhances the sound. Know how to turn off the systems. If they cannot be turned off, change the location of your microphone.

Consider Your Audience

Have you heard the expression: *there is one in every crowd*?
There will always be at least one person who is less than enthusiastic or argumentative.

Negative energy can spread like a virus, so one person choosing to be uninspired can disrupt a group. In virtual presentations, consider who attended and how you reached them. If you seem to be hitting your ideal audience, how did you reach them and what can you do to ensure you do it again? If you felt like you missed the target, who do you want there and how do you reach them?

Learn to Let Go

Treat a presentation like any relationship that has run its course: be mature, learn what you can, and move on. Fixating on a wildly successful presentation or remaining stuck on the presentation that did not work will not move you or your business forward. Every presentation will be different. Plan and deliver each one to your best in the moment and use every presentation as a classroom for the next time.

"Be sincere when you are speaking to your audience.

Remember, you have something important to share but you must respect your audience and be willing to listen and learn"

\- Melissa Kalan

CHPATER 10

NOW IT'S YOUR TURN

"Speech is power: speech is to persuade, to convert, to compel" - Ralph Waldo Emerson.

Imagine for a moment, yes, you're standing at the entrance to heaven, and as you peek in, you realize that this time around, you don't have any regrets. You're looking forward to what's to come, and you're also excited because you've challenged yourself and started learning a new skill. That skill is public speaking, and you're getting better every day, and you keep on learning because it's something you feel can fulfill your purpose in life.

But hold on one moment, how did you get to that point?

That's what I'd like to talk to you about in this chapter. I want to give you practical steps that you can use to reap the benefits of acquiring public speaking skills. The benefits that range from leadership skills, better interpersonal, communication and networking, and confidence. It lies waiting for you, but only if you're willing to take the leap and start doing the work.

My story showed that you could take varied paths, meet many different obstacles along the way, and find your purpose. Perhaps you're at the stage where you've walked down so many paths trying to find the one thing that will help you grow yourself personally, professionally, and build strong, healthy relationships.

Maybe it's learning the skills of public speaking, or perhaps it's not. If it is, then I'll tell you the best way to proceed based on my experience with others in a similar situation. Here's a step by step approach to get started:

Step 1 - Understand the nature of public speaking and what it can do for you and your career or business.

Step 2 - Read this book in its entirety and think back to the question I posed in the introduction. Did you achieve your outcome in reading this book? Did you recognize what was holding you back?

Step 3 - Answer the questions posed above, and if you said yes to both questions, it might be the perfect time to start finding out more about public speaking. How can you do this?

Step 4 - This book is one resource, and there are many others including books that you buy from Amazon, but how long will that take? Perhaps a year or more, depending on your consistency. Ask yourself: Do I have the time to scour online to find the exact process to become a public speaker? If you're comfortable doing so, then you may also pause at this point. If not, then perhaps you're ready to explore other avenues to get this public speaking skill.

Step 5 - Since you know you want to get good at public speaking and you want to be efficient in gaining these skills, it might be a good idea to get coaching in the discipline of public speaking.

Step 6 - Alternatively, you may want to further educate yourself by watching YouTube or other videos that advise you on becoming a better public speaker. Keep in mind this might not always have the most accurate information. Alternatively, you could choose to buy a course that systematically tells you everything you need to know about public speaking, giving you a step by step framework to use and that will help you achieve your goal.

A few years back, I sat in a similar situation, wondering what's the next best step to take. I knew that I needed training, but I wasn't sure which way to proceed. Eventually, I made the call and started learning everything. Still, finally, I started getting expert help from other speakers, and slowly my skills grew, and after some time, I could see marked differences. I discovered that everyone needs some help either at this point or later down the line. Once I started raising my hand and asking for help, that's when my public speaking career skyrocketed.

To conclude, through my own experience, speaking at over 40+ events, I always imagine speaking like I'm talking to one person and a good friend. Whether that is a conference of 600 people, an online virtual event of 1000's, or it's just me and the camera, the camera is my friend.

Some other words of encouragement and advice I would leave you with as someone starting:

- Research and read broadly
- Time, practice, and rehearse out aloud

- Keep to time
- Stay on topic
- Pause and breathe
- Get into character or the zone
- Less is more principle

Last but not least, I would tell you to **Go for it**!
I look forward to seeing you on the stage soon.

To your public speaking success,
Melissa x

About Melissa Kalan

Melissa Kalan is the Founding Director of ARMA - Australian Revenue Management Association, providing online revenue management education to the global accommodation industry and academic partners.

Her life philosophy is centred on the principle of "always learning", and with this she empowers organisations to lead a revenue management culture from the top down that influences both profits and staff retention.

Her background includes revenue management positions within Qantas Airlines domestic and international networks, and The Ritz-Carlton, Hotel Company.

Melissa implemented best-practice techniques at various The Ritz-Carlton properties in the Asia Pacific region and wrote and owns the first nationally online accredited VET short course in revenue management and co-developed the Graduate Certificate of Revenue Management – an online globally recognised qualification, the first of its kind, in a commercial partnership with Torrens University Australia. Melissa co-facilitates the university program with Torrens University Australia.

Melissa has consulted on revenue management projects for organisations such as BIG4 Holiday Parks Australia, Discovery Parks, ALH Group, Majestic Hotels, Wyndham Hotels, Choice Hotels Asia-Pacific and Golden Chain.

ARMA also provides customised e-learning training portals for organisations and e-learning course development.

ARMA is also the preferred supplier of revenue management training for both the Accommodation Association and Tourism Industry Aotearoa.

Melissa is a frequent speaker at conferences on revenue management and founded the APAC Revenue Management Summit held annually in Melbourne and attracts over 200 delegates and 27 partners. This was adapted to a virtual event in 2020.

With a passion for revenue management and always considering herself a "student to the discipline", Melissa has created a fast-growing global network of revenue management focused professionals and organisations.

To further her interest in e-learning and her mission to provide cost effective upskill programs that are engaging and of the highest standard with exceptional student experiences she has expanded ARMA beyond the accommodation industry and launched eSkillsHUB in 2020 providing online certifications in business and personal development.

Speaking Portfolio – Melissa Kalan

VTIC – Victorian Tourism Industry Council, Geelong VIC 2014

Wyndham Hotel Group – Asia Pacific GM conference, Sydney 2014

ARMA Checking in with RM, Adelaide, August 2014

ARMA Checking in with RM, Melbourne, November 2014

Maximum Occupancy industry event, Brisbane QLD Dec 2014

Grand Hotels conference, Brisbane December 2014

Scoopon Travel Sales Managers Meeting, VIC Dec 2014

ARMA Checking in with RM, Western Australia, March 2015

ARMA Checking in with RM, Sydney, March 2015

YesBookIT National Conference, Sydney, May 2015

William Angliss Institute – 75th Anniversary event, June 2015

Choice Hotels Australasia National Conference, August 2015

BIG4 National Conference, Canberra, October 2015

ARMA Checking in with RM, Brisbane, October 2015

Maximum Occupancy, Auckland & Sydney, November 2015

Direct is BEST Master Class, Sydney, April 2016

Marcus Evans Pricing Analytics Conference, Sydney, August 2016

Choice Hotels Australasia Conference, Hobart, August 2016

APAC Revenue Management Summit, Melbourne, Nov 2016

Scoopon Travel Sales Manager Meeting, Melbourne, September 2016

Maximum Occupancy Conference – Sydney, November 2016

Tasmanian Tourism Council Conference - Reimagine, May 2017

New Zealand Hotel Industry Conference, Auckland, July 2017

Top10 Holiday Parks Conference, Christchurch, August 2017

APAC Revenue Management Summit, Melbourne, August 2017

Maximum Occupancy New Zealand, Auckland, September 2017

Golden Chain Group Conference, Cairns, 2017

Maximum Occupancy Conference, Sydney, October 2017

Expedia Sydney Summit, Sydney, November 2017

Accommodation Association Hotel Forum, Adelaide, May 2018

Expedia Partner Summit, Perth, June 2018

New Zealand Hotel Industry Conference, Auckland, July 2018

No Vacancy Trade Show, Sydney, July 2018

APAC Revenue Management Summit, Melbourne, August 2018

VIC Parks National Conference, Victoria, August 2018

Sabre and Cendyn Sydney Forum, August 2018

AHA SA Industry Forum, Port Lincoln, October 2018

BIG4 Holiday Parks National Conference, Adelaide, October 2018

Maximum Occupancy, Sydney, November 2018

Maximum Occupancy, New Zealand 2019

New Zealand Hotel Industry Conference 2019

NoVacancy 2019, International Convention Centre Sydney, July 2019

Sabre DNA Forum, International Convention Centre, July 2019

APAC Revenue Management Summit, Melbourne, August 2019

Ted's Technology Summit, CEO Panel, Sydney, September 2019

Maximum Occupancy Sydney, November 2019

ARMA Revenue Management Virtual Summit, July 2020

AHICE 2020, Hyatt Regency Sydney, September 2020

BIG4 Holiday Parks National Virtual Conference, October 2020

Connect with me

Facebook ™
https://www.facebook.com/arma.revenuemanagement

LinkedIn ™
https://www.linkedin.com/in/melissa-kalan-42611060/

Instagram ™
https://www.instagram.com/arma_revenue_management/

Work with me

The business movement empowering woman to find their voice, own their strengths and sell their message to the world.

https://www.arma-revenuemanagement.com/businesshub

Video Bloopers

References

Davis, Martha, Patrick Fanning, and McKay Matthew. *Messages: The Communication Skills Book.* New Harbinger Publications, 1995.

Decker, Bert. *Communication Skills for Leaders: Deliver a Clear and Consistent Message, 4th Ed.* Axzo Press, 2009.

Gehrt, Jennifer, and Colleen Moffitt. *Strategic Public Relations: 10 Principles to Harness the Power of PR.* Xlibris Corporation, 2012.

Hamilton, Cheryl, and Cordell Parker. *Communicating for Results.* Wadsworth Publishing, 2007.

Taylor, Robert. *Media Interview Techniques: A Complete Guide to Media Training,* Kogan Page, 2015.

Todtfeld, Jess, *Media Secrets: A Media Training Crash Course: Get More Publicity, Look & Feel Your Best AND Convert Interviews Into Web Traffic & Sales. Strategies for TV, Print, Radio & Internet Media,* Bestseller Big Business Publishing, 2016.

Boothman, Nicholas. *How to Make People Like You in 90 Seconds or Less.* Workman Publishing Company, 2000.

Carnegie, Dale. *How to Win Friends and Influence People.* Pocket Books, 1998 (Reprint).

—. *The Quick and Easy Way to Effective Speaking.* Pocket Books, 1990.

Cialdini, Robert. *Influence: The Psychology of Persuasion.* Collins, 2006.

Guffey, Mary Ellen. *Essentials of Business Communication* . South-Western College Pub, 2006.

Humes, James. *Speak Like Churchill, Stand Like Lincoln: 21 Powerful Secrets of History's Greatest Speakers.* Three Rivers Press, 2002.

Osborn, Michael, Randall Osborn, and Suzann Osborn. *Public Speaking (8th Edition).* Allyn & Bacon, 2008.

Stevenson, Doug. *How to Write and Deliver a Dynamite Speech.* Cornelia Press, 2006.

—. *Never Be Boring Again.* Cornelia Press, 2003.

Berkley, Susan. *Speak to Influence.* Campbell Hall Press, 2004.

—. *The Quick and Easy Way to Effective Speaking.* Pocket Books, 1990.

Carnegie, Dale, and Joseph Berg Esenwein. *The Art of Public Speaking*. CreateSpace , 2011.

Stevenson, Doug. *Never Be Boring Again*. Cornelia Press, 2003.

Carnegie, Dale.

—. *Public Speaking for Success*. Tarcher, 2006.

—. *The Quick and Easy Way to Effective Speaking*. Pocket Books, 1990.

Carnegie, Dale, and Joseph Berg Esenwein. *The Art of Public Speaking*. CreateSpace , 2011.

Bandler, Richard. *Get the Life You Want: The Secrets to Quick and Lasting Life Change with Neuro-Linguistic Programming*. Health Communications Inc., 2008.

Bandler, Richard, and John Grinder. *Trance-Formations: Neuro-Linguistic Programming and the Structure of Hypnosis*. Real People, 1981.

Cialdini, Robert. *Influence: Science and Practice (5th Edition)*. Prentice Hall, 2008.

—. *Influence: The Psychology of Persuasion (2nd Edition)*. Collins, 2006.

Cialdini, Robert, Noah Goldstein, and Steve Martin. *Yes! 50 Scientifically Proven Ways To Be Persuasive*. Free Press, 2008.

Godin, Seth. *All Marketers are Liars*. Portfolio Hardcover, 2009.

Bilanich, Bud, and Lydia Ramsey. *Success Tweets For Creating Positive Personal Impact*. Front Row Press, 2011.

Canfield, Jack, and Janet Switzer. *The Success Principles*. William Morrow Paperbacks, 2006.

Fisher, Roger, Bruce Patton, and William Ury. *Getting to Yes*. Penguin, 2011.

Post, Emily, and Peter Post. *Emily Post's The Etiquette Advantage in Business*. William Morrow, 2005.

Wheeler, Alina. *Designing Brand Identity (Third Edition)*. Wiley and Sons, 2009.

Cialdini, Robert, *Pre-Suasion*, Simon and Shuster, 2018

Colgreave, Andy and Jeffrey Shaffer, *The Big Book of Dashboards*, Wiley, 2017

Knaffic, Cole Nussbaumer, *Storytelling with Data,* Wiley, 2015

Lasater, Ike and Julie Stiles, *Words That Work In Business*, PuddleDancer Press, 2010

Lewis, David, *Effective Communication in the Workplace*, Kindle Edition

Morin, Christophe and Patrick Renvoise, *The Persuasion Code*, Wiley, 2018

Benjamin, Susan F. *Perfect Phrases for Dealing with Difficult Situations at Work*. McGraw-Hill, 2008.

Blanchard, Ken, and Sheldon Bowles. *High Five! The Magic of Working Together*. William Morrow, 2000.

Cava, Roberta. *Difficult People*. Key Porter Books, 1992.

Gitomer, Jeffery. *Little Black Book of Connections: 6.5 Assets for Networking Your Way to Rich Relationships* . Bard Press, 2006.

Hamilton, Cheryl, and Cordell Parker. *Communicating for Results*. Wadsworth Publishing, 2007.

Kemp, Sid. *Perfect Solutions for Difficult Employee Situations*. McGraw-Hill, 2004.

Lamott, Ann, and Geneen Roth. *When You Eat at the Refrigerator, Pull Up a Chair*. Hyperion, 1999.

Pan, Yuling, Ronald Scollon, and Suzanne Wong Scollon. *Professional Communication in International Settings*. Blackwell Publishing Limited, 2002.

Patterson, Kerry, Joseph Grenny, Ron McMillan, and Al Switzler. *Crucial Confrontations: Tools for Resolving Broken Promises, Violated Expectations, and Bad Behavior*. McGraw-Hill, 2005.

—. *Crucial Conversations: Tools for Talking When Stakes are High*. McGraw-Hill: 2002.

www.ingramcontent.com/pod-product-compliance
Lightning Source LLC
Chambersburg PA
CBHW060009050426
42448CB00012B/2673